beautiful
Beaded
Embroidery

PUBLISHING

First published in North America by
C&T Publishing Inc., PO Box 1456, Lafayette, CA 94549

Text and Artwork ©2006 Country Bumpkin Publications

PUBLISHER
Amy Marson, C&T Publishing, Inc.

EDITOR
Marian Carpenter

EDITORIAL ASSISTANTS
Anna Scott, Heather Moody

GRAPHIC DESIGNERS
Ann Jefferies, Jenny James

PATTERN DESIGNERS
Sarah Kent, Kathy Barac

ILLUSTRATIONS
Kathy Barac

PHOTOGRAPHY
Andrew Dunbar

10 9 8 7 6 5 4 3 2 1

ISBN: 10 digit: 1-57120-406-7
13 digit: 978-1-57120-406-6

Printed in China

For a list of other fine books from C&T Publishing, ask for a free catalog:
C&T Publishing, Inc.
P.O. Box 1456, Lafayette, CA 94549
Phone: (800) 284-1114   **Email:** ctinfo@ctpub.com
Website: www.ctpub.com

For quilting supplies:
Cotton Patch Mail Order
3405 Hall Lane, Dept. CTB, Lafayette, CA 94549
Phone: (800) 835-4418 or (925) 283-7883   **Email:** quiltusa@yahoo.com
Website: www.quiltusa.com

A Brief History of Beading

Over the centuries, beads have been used as symbols to denote love, wealth and status, and often acted as currency to bribe or barter. In some cultures they are credited with magical properties. They are viewed as lucky charms and are often used to ward off evil spirits.

The tradition of threading objects on a length of fiber was practised long before the Ice Age. Seeds, beans, berries and shells in their natural state were some of the first beads used. Later, shells and stones were ground and drilled. In recent times, archeologists, while excavating Stone Age grave sites in Israel, have discovered traces of head dresses that are elaborately embroidered with beads made of broken bones and shells from the Mediterranean Sea. Flat, disc shaped beads of shell, stone and pottery have been found in Egyptian mummy cases.

EUROPE

During the Middle Ages, glass beads were manufactured in Venice. The first glass manufacturing houses were set up in London in 1549 and a glass industry operated in Amsterdam between 1608 and 1680 supplying the needs of the Dutch East India Company as a trading commodity. Beads of blue, yellow and green were popular, with red used less frequently as this color was expensive.

In the 18th century, beaded bags were popular in France. They featured closely packed beading, reportedly using 165 per square centimeter.

Long before the 19th century, beads were used in various parts of Europe, where they embellished vestments and hangings in cathedrals and churches. During the 1850's beadwork was combined with wool embroidery on canvas, as in Berlin work. Each bead took the place of a single tent stitch. A tonal beadwork style, known as Grisaille work, featured clear beads together with beads of white, black and shades of grey. The designs were often pictorial and it was common to leave the background unworked.

NORTH AMERICA

Early native American beadwork used seeds, shells, carved bone and minerals which were all stitched to form surface decoration on clothing. Similar in appearance to present day bugle beads, purple and white cylinders, called wampum, were cut from mussel shells. They were threaded onto sinews to form short rows which were attached by the ends. This technique was called lazy squaw stitch. An alternative method suited to curves or outlines, was to secure the row by couching along the sinew.

In the 17th century, with the migration of settlers and the establishment of a colony in Virginia, the native Americans were exposed to the colorful beads that were traded. Their style of embroidery was influenced by the Spanish and French nuns in convents and missionary schools.

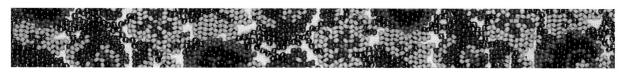

Belgian beaded bag and detail of Ukrainian shirt (c1920's) courtesy of the museum of The Embroiderers' Guild of South Australia.

CONTENTS

6 THE BEADED FLOWER
An exquisite flower exploring the
technique of beading

10 PEARLS OF WISDOM
Fiery beaded dragons worked on satin
dancing slippers

14 DARE TO DREAM
Gorgeous silk cushion covered with
roses and pearls

18 NOSTALGIA
Exquisite silk and lace evening purse
with ribbon flowers

26 SILKEN TOUCH
Elegant little strawberries trimmed with
crystals and embroidery

30 GLAD TIDINGS
Sophisticated Christmas tree decoration

34 ANTIQUE GOLD
Lavishly beaded evening bag

40 BERRY DELIGHT
Miniature berries decorate the lids of
tiny trinket pots

48   VEIL OF GOLD
Opulent beauty created with gold, pearls
and crystals

52   WINTER LOVE
Stunning ring cushion with beads and bows

60   GLITTERING DREAMS
Cardigan richly embellished with beads,
sequins and rhinestones

64   CAPRICE
Exotic embroidered evening bag with
beads and sequins

74   REJOICE
A perfect decoration for the festive season

84   TAKING TEA
Amazing beaded teapot picture

92   RARE VINTAGE
Exquisite beaded evening bag

100   KEEPSAKE
Gorgeous beaded drawstring bag, garter
and horseshoe

106   PURPLE PASSION
Beautiful smocked and beaded bag

110   CONSTRUCTION

128   STEP-BY-STEP INDEX

— THE —
BEADED
FLOWER

by ANNA SCOTT of SOUTH AUSTRALIA

*This exquisite design was created with the purpose of exploring
the exciting technique of beading. The finished piece could be framed,
incorporated into other works or used to embellish
box lids, small bags, home furnishings - almost anything!*

REQUIREMENTS

Fabric

25cm (10") square of pale yellow silk dupioni

Supplies

25cm (10") square of medium weight woven fusible interfacing

Machine sewing thread to match the silk dupioni

Tracing paper

Sharp lead pencil

15cm (6") embroidery hoop

Beads, Sequins, Cord & Needle

See this page.

PREPARATION FOR EMBROIDERY

See the liftout pattern for the embroidery design.

Preparing the fabric

Fuse the interfacing to the wrong side of the silk dupioni fabric. Neaten all edges with a machine zigzag or overlock stitch.

Transferring the design

Using a black pen, trace the design onto the tracing paper. Tape the tracing to a window or light box.

With the right side of the fabric facing up, place it over the tracing, aligning the straight grain of the fabric with the placement marks. Tape the fabric in place. The light shining through will make the design easy to see. Using the pencil, trace the flower design.

THIS DESIGN USES

Lazy squaw stitch
Couched beads
Overlapping sequins

EMBROIDERY

See pages 8 and 9 for the step-by-step instructions for attaching the beads and sequins.

See the liftout pattern for the stitch direction diagram.

The embroidery is worked with the fabric in the hoop.

Order of work

Center

Work a circle of overlapping sequins, along the marked line. Stitch the large gold bead, together with a small red bead, at the center of the sequins.

Padded rim

Cut a 7.5cm (3") length of cord and overcast the ends to prevent fraying. Lay the cord along the marked circle and couch in place. Cover the cord with repeating rows of brown, gold and red beads, angled around the circle. The beads will be very close together inside the circle and fanned out on the outside.

Gold petals

Beginning at the padded rim and working towards the tip, outline one side of the first petal with a string of bugle beads. Couch in place between each bead. Repeat for the second side. Attach a crystal bead, together with a red bead, at the tip of the petal. Place them in the small gap between the bugle beads. Repeat for the remaining gold petals.

Using the stitch direction diagram as a guide, fill the three petals with rows of gold beads attached with lazy squaw stitch. Couch the center of each row to hold the beads in place.

Brown petals

Work the three brown petals in the same manner, noting the change in stitch direction.

BEADS, SEQUINS, CORD & NEEDLE

Gütermann 6mm (1/4") bead
A = no. 2885 gold (1 bead)
Olaf size 9 seed beads
B = no. 22 gold
C = no. 25 Christmas red
Olaf size 10 seed beads
D = brown siam
Bicone Swarovski crystals 4mm (3/16") wide
E = burgundy (6 beads)
Bugle beads 4mm (3/16") long
F = bronze-gold
Laser cup sequins 6mm (1/4") diameter
G = gold
Cord
H = 10cm (4") length of gold lacing cord
Needle
Fine beading needle

EMBROIDERY KEY

All beading is worked with two strands of machine sewing thread.

Center surround = G (overlapped sequins)

Center = A attached with C

Padded rim = H (laid and couched), B, C and D (lazy squaw stitch)

Gold petals

Outline = F (couched lazy squaw stitch)

Tip = E and C (individually attached)

Filling = B (lazy squaw stitch)

Brown petals

Outline = F (couched lazy squaw stitch)

Tip = E and C (individually attached)

Filling = D (lazy squaw stitch)

THE FINISHED EMBROIDERY MEASURES 9CM X 8CM WIDE (3 1/2" X 3 1/4").

ATTACHING BEADS

Beads can be attached singly, in rows, as a string or in combinations of beads. We used contrasting cord and thread for photographic purposes.

INDIVIDUALLY SEWN BEAD

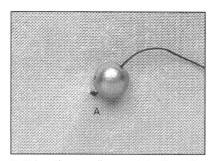

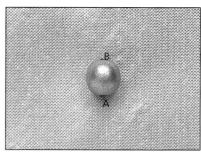

1. Bring the needle up at A. Place the bead onto the needle. Slide the bead down the thread and settle it in place.

2. Leaving a space the same size as the bead, take the needle to the back at B and secure with a back stitch.

ATTACHING WITH A SECOND BEAD

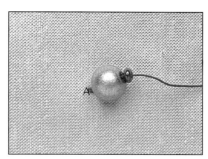

1. Bring the needle up at A. Thread large bead. Thread a smaller bead and slide it down onto the first bead.

2. Take the needle back through the first bead, then to back of the work close to A. Secure with a back stitch.

LAZY SQUAW STITCH

1. Bring the needle up at A. Thread the required number of beads and settle them in place.

2. Take the needle to the back at B, allowing beads to lie comfortably, and secure with a back stitch.

COUCHED BEADS

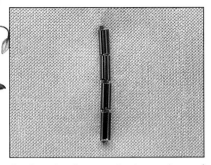

1. Attach the required number of beads following instructions for lazy squaw stitch, allowing a small space between each bead.

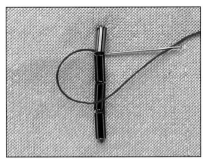

2. Bring the thread to the front between the first and second bead. Work a straight stitch over the thread between each of the beads.

COUCHED BEADS OVER A CORD

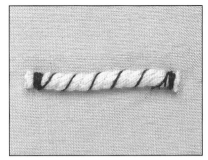

1. Lay the cord onto the fabric and couch in place using matching thread.

COUCHED BEADS OVER A CORD

2. Bring the thread to the front at A, just beside the edge of the cord. Thread five beads onto the cord and settle them in place.

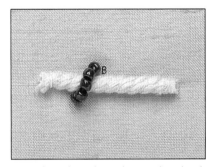

3. Take the thread to the back at B, diagonally on the opposite side of the cord.

4. Secure on the back with a back stitch. Continue attaching beads in repeating rows over the cord.

OVERLAPPING SEQUINS

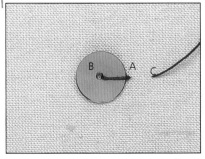

1. Attach the first sequin with a back stitch beginning at A, going down through the center at B and emerging at C, half a sequin away.

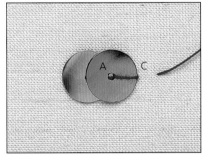

2. Place the next sequin to overlap the first. Work a back stitch coming up at C and down through the center of the second sequin at A.

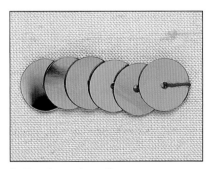

3. Continue along the row.

PEARLS OF WISDOM

by DANA COX of QUEENSLAND

These dazzling designs are worked on slippers made of black satin.
The slippers are tied around the ankles with elegant royal blue satin ribbons.

REQUIREMENTS

1 pair of black satin dancing slippers

4m x 35mm wide (4yd 14 " x 1 ³/₈") royal blue double sided satin ribbon

White dressmaker's carbon eg Saral

Tracing paper

Tissue paper

Fine black permanent pen

Threads, Beads & Needles

See page 12.

We recommend that you read the complete article and instructions in the liftout pattern relating to this project before you begin.

PREPARATION FOR EMBROIDERY

See the liftout pattern for the embroidery designs.

Transferring the designs

Using the pen, trace each dragon design for the toe of each slipper onto separate pieces of tracing paper and cut out, leaving a 2.5cm (1") border around each design.

Tightly fill the toe of each slipper with tissue paper. Cut two pieces of carbon the same size as the tracings. Position the traced design onto the matching toe of one slipper and tape one side of the design to the slipper *(diag 1).*

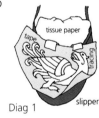

Diag 1

Slide the carbon under the tracing, ensuring the carbon side is against the slipper *(diag 2).*

Diag 2

Lightly tape the other side of the tracing. Using a ball point pen and pressing firmly, trace all design lines. Remove the tracing paper and carbon. Repeat for the toe of the remaining slipper.

Trace the cloud symbols for the inner and outer sides of the slippers twice, in the same manner as the toes and cut out, leaving a 1.5cm (⁵/₈") border around each design.

Tightly fill the remainder of each slipper with tissue paper. Cut four pieces of carbon to the same size as the tracings. Transfer the designs in the same manner as the toe designs.

EMBROIDERY

See page 13 for step-by-step instructions for attaching beads.

The dragon bodies and legs are first outlined in metallic thread and then beaded. Metallic threads are used for the heads, feet and tails. The eyes are beaded and the tongues are worked in rayon thread. The Chinese cloud symbols are worked in metallic thread.

Work through the layer of black satin only. Keep the stitching surface and the angle of the needle as flat as possible *(diag 3).*

Diag 3

Use two strands of gold thread for all the gold embroidery and three or four strands of the coloured metallic threads. One strand of stranded rayon is used for the tongue.

All embroidery is worked using the milliner's needle. The beads are attached with the beading thread and the no. 12 sharp needle.

Order of work

Fiery dragons

Following the close-up photograph, diagrams and embroidery key, work all the outlines in stem stitch first. Work the snouts and tongues in satin stitch.

Securely attach the beads, starting at the neck and following the curves of the outlines as a guide.

Chinese cloud symbols

Using two strands of metallic thread, begin stitching on an inner curl and work in stem stitch around the shape, finishing at the corresponding curl.

End off the thread securely.

Repeat for all the remaining cloud symbols.

CONSTRUCTION

See page 110.

THE FINISHED DRAGONS MEASURE 5.5CM X 9CM WIDE (3 ¹/₂" X 2 ¹/₄").

Step 1

Step 2

THREADS, BEADS & NEEDLES

Madeira no. 5 metallic thread
A = 5012 bright gold
B = 5014 black-gold
C = 5017 gold
Madeira no. 10 metallic thread
D = 0312 purple
E = 0315 red
F = 0338 royal blue
G = 0357 green
H = 0370 harlequin
Madeira metallic sewing thread no.40
I = 37 turquoise
Anchor Marlitt stranded rayon
J = 1017 red
Mill Hill glass seed beads
K = 00020 royal blue
L = 00283 mercury
M = 00358 cobalt blue
N = 00367 garnet
O = 00374 rainbow
P = 00556 antique silver
Mill Hill antique beads
Q = 03035 royal green
R = 03037 abalone
Mill Hill petite beads
S = 40557 yellow gold
T = 42030 rose gold
Mill Hill bugle beads 6mm (¹/₄")
U = 72011 gold
Needles
No. 5 milliner's
No. 12 sharp

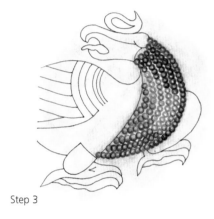

Step 3

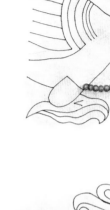

Step 4

EMBROIDERY COLOR KEY

 A    F
 B   G
C   H
 D   I
 E   J

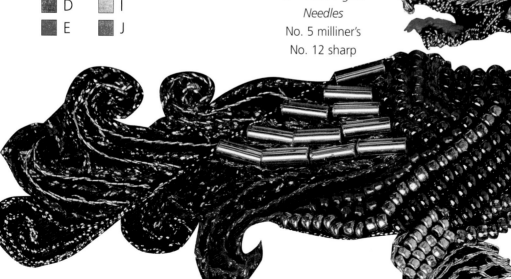

Right slipper

Step 1

ATTACHING BEADS

Each bead is attached to the fabric using a back stitch. This is a particularly secure method of attaching beads as the thread passes through each bead twice.

Step 2

1. Bring the needle to the front at A. Thread a bead onto the needle. Take a tiny back stitch from B to A, under the bead.

2. Pull the thread through. Take the thread through the bead again. Thread on a second bead.

3. Take a tiny back stitch under the second bead, then take the thread through the bead. Continue in the same manner until the required number of beads is stitched in place.

Step 4

Step 3

4. To end off, take the needle to the back and secure with a back stitch.

BEADING COLOR KEY

K   N   Q   T
L   O   R   U
M   P   S

Left slipper

DARE TO DREAM

by JULIE GRAUE of QUEENSLAND

"I love roses above all flowers and I try to incorporate them into all of my embroidery. When I found this gorgeous cream silk, I knew it would go perfectly with roses and pearls. The soft pinks of the roses have made this pretty cushion totally feminine."

~ JULIE ~

REQUIREMENTS

Fabric

35cm x 40cm wide (13 ¾" x 15 ¾") piece of ivory silk dupioni

90cm x 135cm wide (35 ½" x 53 ⅛") shell pink silk dupioni

Threads, Beads & Needles

See page 16.

Supplies

1.1m (1yd 7") baby pink mini piping

2 x 19mm (¾") wide self cover buttons

Polyester fiber-fill

Water-soluble fabric marker

PREPARATION FOR EMBROIDERY

See the liftout pattern for the pintucking template.

Preparing the fabric

Cut a 31.6cm (12 ½") square from the ivory silk dupioni. Neaten the raw edges with a machine zigzag or overlock stitch. With the right side uppermost and aligning the raw edges of the fabric with the marked lines on the template, place the left half of the fabric over the pintucking template. Pin in place to prevent movement.

Using the water-soluble fabric marker and a ruler, trace the diagonal lines onto

THIS DESIGN USES

Back stitch · Beading
Bullion knot · Bullion loop
Detached chain
French knot · Pintucking

the fabric. Remove the pins. Position the remaining half of the fabric over the template, matching the lines with those on the previous half of the square.

Pin the fabric in place and rule these lines in the same manner as before.

Pintucking the cushion front

With wrong sides together, fold the fabric along one ruled line and press. Using machine sewing thread to match the fabric, stitch 1.5mm (¹/₁₆") from the fold along the entire length. Repeat the procedure along all the remaining lines in the same direction. Work pintucks along all the lines in the opposite direction in the same manner.

Rinse the pintucked fabric under cold running water to remove all traces of the fabric marker.

Pin the fabric to an ironing board, pulling it into a square shape. Leave until dry. Press, ensuring the square shape is retained.

Marking design placements

Place a ruler across the center pintucked diamond from corner to corner. Using the fabric marker, mark the midpoint of the diamond with a small dot. Excluding the outer row of complete diamonds, mark the centers of the remaining diamonds in the same manner.

EMBROIDERY

Each floral posy is embroidered in the same manner. Stitch a posy at each marked dot, except in the diamond at the very center.

Use the milliner's needle for all embroidery and for attaching the beads.

Order of Work

Roses

Beginning 1.5mm (¹/₁₆") from the marked center of a diamond, stitch a bullion loop for the center of the rose. Ensure the loop lies over the center mark. Using the same thread, work three overlapping bullion knots for the inner petals. Change thread color and surround the inner petals with five overlapping bullion knots.

Leaves

Embroider four pairs of detached chain leaves around the rose. Position them so they point towards the corners of the diamond.

"This is one of my favourite pieces of work and was such a pleasure to create."

~ JULIE ~

Forget-me-nots

Stitch a forget-me-knot between each pair of leaves. Work three blue French knots in a triangle for the petals and add a yellow French knot for the center.

Clusters of beads

Attach a cream bead in each corner of the embroidered diamonds to form a cluster, omitting the diamonds at the outer edge. After each cluster is secured, take the thread through each bead and pull firmly. Secure the thread on the back of the fabric. This will hold the cluster together.

At the intersections around the outer edge, three beads will be attached in the same manner. However, these beads are not attached until the cushion is partially assembled.

CONSTRUCTION

See pages 110 - 112.
See opposite for step-by-step instructions for creating the beaded button.

THREADS, BEADS AND NEEDLES

Anchor stranded cotton

A = 128 vy lt delft blue

B = 858 lt fern green

C = 892 ultra lt shell pink

D = 893 vy lt shell pink

DMC stranded cotton

E = 745 vy lt yellow

Mill Hill glass seed beads

F = 00123 cream

No. 9 milliner's needle

Doll needle

EMBROIDERY KEY

All embroidery is worked with two strands of thread unless otherwise specified.

Roses

Center = D (bullion loop, 15 wraps)

Inner petals = D (3 bullion knots 12 wraps)

Outer petals = C (5 bullion knots 12 wraps)

Leaves = B (detached chain)

Forget-me-nots

Petals = A (French knot, 1 wrap)

Center = E (French knot 1 wrap)

Clusters of beads = F (beading)

Hints

1. Use a long, thin needle as some beads have very small holes. Milliner's and 'sharp' needles are commonly used and are most suitable.

2. Polyester sewing machine thread is a strong, fine thread perfect for attaching beads.

3. Use stitches that are exactly the same length as the bead. A stitch that is too long will allow the bead to move and one that is too short will prevent the bead from lying securely against the fabric.

THE FINISHED CUSHION, INCLUDING THE FRILL, MEASURES 47CM (18 ½") SQUARE.

BEADED BUTTON

Tiny seed beads are used to transform a simple self cover button into an opulent centerpiece on the cushion.

We used contrasting thread and beads for photographic purposes.

"Applying the beading takes patience but I found it easier to work in a clockwise direction." ~ JULIE

1. Using matching machine sewing thread, anchor the thread to the fabric on the edge of the button with two tiny back stitches.

2. Place a bead onto the needle and slide it down to the fabric. Take a back stitch the same length as the bead near the edge of the button.

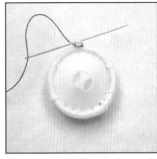

3. Pull the thread through. Take the needle back through the bead.

4. Pull the thread through. Place a second bead onto the needle and slide it down to the fabric.

5. Secure the bead as close as possible to the previous bead in the same manner as before.

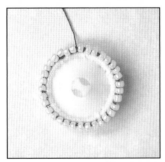

6. Continue securing beads around the edge of the button until reaching the beginning.

7. Attach a second round of beads beside the first, keeping them as close as possible.

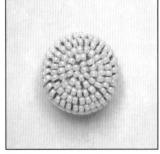

8. Continue attaching rounds of beads until the fabric is completely covered. End off the thread with two tiny back stitches. **Completed beaded button.**

– THE HISTORY OF BUTTONS –

*P*recious metals, gems and ivory have been used for buttons, but most buttons are made of such materials as wood, glass, mother-of-pearl, bone, horn, brass, pewter, and plastics. Buttons have been worn as ornaments since the Bronze Age, and were sometimes used as fasteners by the Greeks and Romans. They became popular in Europe in the 13th and 14th centuries when form-fitted clothing came into fashion. In the 16th century, wearing buttons became a means of displaying wealth, and many buttons were set with diamonds and other gems. In the 18th century fine, handcrafted buttons were made of painted porcelain, tortoiseshell inlay, ivory and engraved gems. Embroidered and brass buttons were also popular. Nowadays, buttons are primarily mass-produced in plastic. The collecting of fine antique buttons is a popular hobby.

NOSTALGIA

An elegant evening bag designed by

DEBORAH WEST BANGS of COLORADO, USA

REQUIREMENTS

Fabric & Lace

25cm x 60cm wide (9 $\frac{7}{8}$" x 23 $\frac{3}{4}$")
piece of 100% raw silk

25cm x 60cm wide (9 $\frac{7}{8}$" x 23 $\frac{3}{4}$")
piece of gold satin for lining

30cm (11 $\frac{3}{4}$") square of silk metallic
Chantilly lace with a scalloped edge

Ribbons, Threads, Beads & Needles

See page 22.

Supplies

90cm x 6mm wide (35 $\frac{1}{2}$" x $\frac{1}{4}$")
burgundy and gold braid

5cm x 13cm wide (2" x 5") purse frame

59cm (23 $\frac{1}{4}$") long purse chain

20cm (8") square of medium
weight buckram

20cm (8") square of lightweight
interfacing for transferring the floral
design

Water-soluble fabric marker

Sharp lead pencil

Black pen

Jewelry pliers

THIS DESIGN USES

Appliqué · Beading · Couching
Folded ribbon rose
Gathered ribbon techniques

PATTERN & CUTTING OUT

*See the liftout pattern for the cutting
layout and pattern.*

Trace the pattern piece and all markings
onto lightweight interfacing or tracing
paper. Cut out the purse shape from the
silk and the lining, transferring the
markings. With the water-soluble fabric
marker, mark the front of the silk at the
positions for the top and bottom of the
embroidery design with small dots.
Aligning the scalloped edge of the lace
with the marking on the pattern, cut out
the lace for the front.

PREPARATION FOR EMBROIDERY

*See the liftout pattern for the embroidery
design and flower placement guide.*

Transferring the design to the buckram

Using the lead pencil, trace the flower
and leaf placement marks onto the
square of lightweight interfacing.
Centering the design, place the
interfacing over the buckram and pin in
place to prevent movement. Using the
black pen and pressing firmly enough to
pierce the interfacing, mark the buckram
with the flower and leaf positions.
Remove the tracing.

Purse

Using the fabric marker, mark each
beading position along the foldline on
the silk at the positions indicated on the
pattern. This is the base of the purse.

Mounting the lace

Lay the silk out flat with the right side of
the fabric facing up.

Place the lace, right side up, over the
front of the purse. Ensure the raw edges
are aligned around the curved edge.
Leaving the scalloped edge of the
lace free and using small stitches,
tack the lace to the fabric
around the remaining three
sides within the seam allowance.
Treat the lace and silk as one layer
when attaching the embroidery and
assembling the purse.

"My project was inspired by the beautiful roses in my grandmother's rose garden." DEBORAH

EMBROIDERY

See pages 22 - 25 for step-by-step instructions for making a wild rose, cabochon rose, continuous petal flower and a mitered ribbon leaf.

The ribbon flowers and leaves are fashioned and applied to the buckram before the design is appliquéd to the front of the purse.

Use the milliner's needle for the ribbon work and appliqué. Use the beading needle for attaching the beads.

Order of work

Cabochon roses

One cabochon rose is positioned towards the top and a group of three nestle near the base of the spray.

Each rose is formed using two types of ribbon. The center is a folded ribbon rose and the three petals are created separately and attached around the center. Fashion the four roses following the instructions on pages 24 - 25.

Wild rose

The wild rose is placed between the single cabochon rose and the group of three. It is formed from four types of ribbon. The flower has a center surrounded by eight separate petals which are attached in three rounds. Work the rose following the instructions on page 23.

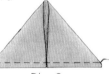

Rosebuds

There are three rosebuds in the spray. Cut a 5cm (2") length of 40mm (1 ½") ribbon for the center. Roll firmly and handstitch. Cut a 5cm (2") length of ribbon for the outer petal. Form the petal in the same manner as a cabochon rose. Wrap the petal around the center and stitch through the base to secure.

Form the calyx using a 4cm (1 ½") length of I. Fold the ribbon in half with the raw ends together and wrap the rectangle of ribbon around the bud. Handstitch the ends together.

Large continuous petal flower

This flower is located below the group of cabochon roses. Cut a 19cm (7 ½") length of ribbon. Form the flower following the step-by-step instructions on page 25.

Small continuous petal flowers

Form two smaller flowers in the same manner as the large flower, again following the instructions on page 25. Use a 13cm (5 ⅛") length of ribbon for each flower.

Gathered ribbon flowers

Work two gathered flowers using the satin edged georgette ribbon. Cut the ribbon in half. Fold the ribbon lengthwise with the satin edges lying side by side *(see diag 1)*.

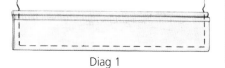

Diag 1

Beginning and ending at the satin edges, work running stitches across the ends and along the folded edge *(diag 1)*. Pull up the running stitches to gather the ribbon and join into a circle. Stitch a single gold bead at the center.

Folded ribbon leaves

Cut two pieces of J, K and L each 7cm (2 ¾") in length. Mark the center of one piece of ribbon with a pin. Fold over each half of the ribbon diagonally. Using small stitches, handstitch a row of running stitch through both layers along the lower edge *(diag 2)*. Pull up the running stitch and secure the thread. Repeat for the remaining lengths of ribbon.

Diag 2

Cut the length of N into three equal pieces. Form three more leaves in the same manner.

Mitered ribbon leaves

Cut one piece each of E, F and H 13cm (5 ⅛") long. Cut two pieces each of J and L and one piece each of J and K, 10cm (4") long. Form the leaves following the step-by-step instructions on page 22.

Attaching the flowers to the buckram

Pin the flowers onto the piece of buckram at the marked positions. Tack the wild rose in place first, taking the stitches well under the flower. Working

THE FINISHED EVENING PURSE MEASURES 26.5CM X 21CM WIDE (10 ½" X 8 ¼") EXCLUDING FRINGE.

from the center to the outside of the design, secure the cabochon roses and then the remaining flowers. Add the two stems for the buds on the left hand side, securing them at each end only. Stitch the buds and leaves to the floral arrangement.

When the embroidery is secure, cut away the excess buckram from around the flowers, trimming as close as possible so the buckram will not show. Entirely cut away the buckram from beneath the stems. The remaining buckram acts as support for the design once it is sewn onto the purse.

Appliquéing the arrangement

Place the arrangement over the lace, matching the gathered ribbon flowers with the marked positions. Handstitch the buckram to the purse beneath the

flowers. Using threads to match the flowers and leaves, work hidden stitches to catch all edges of the flowers, leaves, buds and stems so they stay secure.

Fringe

Attach the first and last string of beads after the side seams have been stitched. Using the beading needle, secure a doubled thread at the marked position for the second string of beads. Slip two gold beads, a faceted oval, a gold bead, a leaf and finally a seed bead (which is the anchor), onto the needle. Pull the thread through. Omitting the seed bead, pass the needle and thread back through the leaf and subsequent beads and emerge on the wrong side of the fabric (diag 3). Diag 3 Take several small stitches to secure before moving to the next beading position in the sequence.

CONSTRUCTION
See pages 112 - 113.

RIBBONS, THREADS, BEADS & NEEDLES

Note: some ribbons are substitutes as the originals are unavailable.

No. 4546 Mokuba satin edged crepe georgette ribbon 15mm (⁵⁄₈") wide

A = 20cm (8") no. 15 gold

No. 4599 Mokuba shot rayon ribbon 23mm (1") wide

B = 80cm (31 ½") no. 15 burgundy/blue

No. 4599 Mokuba shot rayon ribbon 13mm (½") wide

C = 25cm (10") no. 15 burgundy/blue

Cut edge organza ribbon 25mm (1") wide

D = 60cm (23 ½") rust

No. 4070 French wire-edged shot rayon ribbon 40mm (1 ½") wide

E = 60cm (23 ½") no. 021 verdigris
F = 60cm (23 ½") no. 295 copper

No. 1482 French 'Mesh Ombre' wire-edged variegated ribbon 40mm (1 ½") wide

G = 60cm (23 ½") no. 8 sunset

No. 20830 French wire-edged rayon ribbon 40mm (1 ½") wide

H = 60cm (23 ½") no. 117 desert sand

No. 1505 Mokuba rayon ribbon 10mm (³⁄₈") wide

I = 15cm (6") no. 15 camel

No. 930 French wire-edged shot rayon ribbon 25mm (1") wide

J = 40cm (15 ¾") no. 721 dark green
K = 30cm (11 ¾") no. 889 khaki green

RST25 French wire-edged rayon ribbon 25mm (1") wide

L = 40cm (15 ¾") no. 892 olive green

No. 4000 Mokuba double faced velvet ribbon 3mm (¹⁄₈") wide

M = 15cm (6") no. 16 fuzzy green

Metallic ribbon 15mm (⁵⁄₈") wide

N = 25cm (9 ¾") gold

O = 50 gold beads 3mm (¹⁄₈") wide

P = 15 amber oval faceted beads 8mm (³⁄₈") long

Q = 15 clear gold trimmed leaf beads 13mm (½") long

R = 1 rose bead 5mm (³⁄₁₆") wide

Mill Hill frosted glass seed beads

S = no. 62057 khaki

No. 9 milliner's needle
No. 10 beading needle

EMBROIDERY KEY

Cabochon roses

Rose 1
Center = D (folded rose)
Outer petals = G (rolled edge, gathering)

Rose 2
Center = B (folded rose)
Outer petals = H (rolled edge, gathering)

Rose 3
Center = D (folded rose)
Outer petals = F
(rolled edge, gathering)

Rose 4
Center = B (folded rose)
Outer petals = E
(rolled edge, gathering)

Wild rose
Center = F (folded rose)
Inner petals = G (rolled edge, pleating)
Middle petals = E (rolled edge, pleating)
Outer petals = H (rolled edge, pleating)

Rosebuds
Center = B or D (rolled ribbon)
Petal = G (rolled edge, gathering)
Calyx = I (wrapping)
Stem = M (couching)

Large continuous petal flower
Petals = B (gathering)
Center = R (beading)

Small continuous petal flowers
Petals = C (gathering)
Center = S (beading)

Gathered ribbon flowers
Petals = A (gathering)
Center = O (beading)

Folded ribbon leaves
Leaves = J, K, L or N (folding, gathering)

Mitered ribbon leaves
Leaves = E, F, H, J, K or L
(mitering, gathering)

Fringe = O, P, Q and S (beading)

MITERED RIBBON LEAF

We used contrasting thread for photographic purposes.

1. Fold the length of ribbon in half.

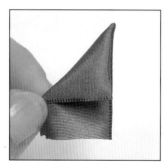

2. Folding diagonally, lay the folded edge so it aligns with the finished edges of the ribbon.

3. Back stitch close to the diagonal fold through all four layers.

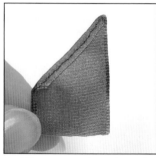

4. Trim away the triangular shape below the stitching.

5. Finger press the seam open. It becomes the vein of the leaf. Stitch tiny running stitches across both pieces of ribbon at the widest point.

6. Pull up the running stitches to gather the ribbon and create the roundness at the base of the leaf.

7. Tie off the gathering thread securely. Trim the tails of ribbon to 5mm ($^3/_{16}$"").

8. Tuck the tails under the leaf. **Completed mitered ribbon leaf.**

WILD ROSE

This rose is formed with a rolled ribbon center and three layers of petals. There are three inner, three middle and two outer petals.

We used contrasting ribbons and threads for photographic purposes.

1. Center. Using a 20cm (8") length of 40mm (1 ½") wide ribbon, form the center following steps 1 - 13 for the cabochon rose.

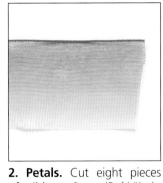

2. Petals. Cut eight pieces of ribbon 8cm (3 ⅛") in length, one for each petal. Remove the wire from each edge of the ribbon.

3. Fold one length of ribbon in half with the raw edges together. The fold becomes the top of the petal.

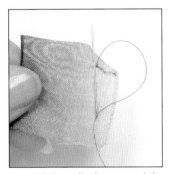

4. Tightly roll the top right hand corner diagonally towards you for two tight rolls. Secure with 2 - 3 small stitches.

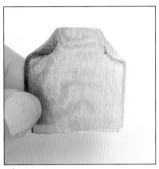

5. Tightly roll the remaining corner in the same manner and hand stitch to secure.

6. At the lower edge form a 6mm (¼") pleat on the front of one half. Handstitch to secure.

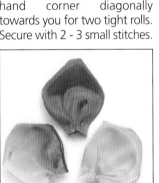

7. Repeat step 6 on the remaining half.

8. Form the remaining seven petals following steps 3 - 7.

9. Position one inner petal around the center and secure it with several tiny stitches through the base.

10. Attach the two remaining inner petals in the same manner.

11. Secure first petal of the second layer in the same manner. Ensure the middle of the petal is positioned behind the sides of two inner petals.

12. Secure the two remaining middle petals in the same manner.

13. Attach the two outer petals, one on each side of the rose. Trim the base.

14. Completed wild rose.

CABOCHON ROSE

Cut a 25cm (9 ¾") length of ribbon for the center. Cut three 6.5cm (2 ½") lengths of ribbon for the petals.

Thread a needle with matching sewing thread before you begin.

For photographic purposes we used contrasting ribbon and thread.

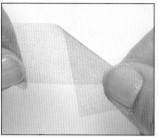

1. Center. Hold the ribbon horizontally in your left hand. Fold over the right hand end of the ribbon diagonally.

2. Still holding the ribbon in your left hand, fold the point over to the left.

3. Roll the ribbon to the left for two turns.

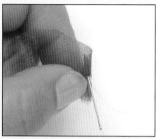

4. Using matching sewing thread, take three stitches through all layers of ribbon at the lower edge.

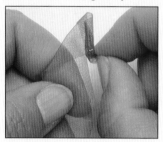

5. Leave the needle hanging. Hold the center in your right hand. Fold the top edge of the ribbon back and down.

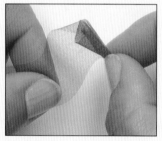

6. Roll the center onto the folded ribbon, keeping the base of the center level with the lower edge of unfolded ribbon.

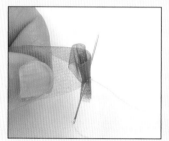

7. Pick up the hanging needle. Take several stitches through all layers at the base. Pull the thread firmly.

8. Leave the needle hanging. Fold the top edge of the ribbon back and down as before.

9. Following steps 6 and 7, wrap the folded ribbon around the center and secure.

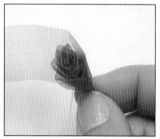

10. Continue as for steps 5 - 7 until 5cm (2") of ribbon remains.

11. Fold the ribbon back and down. Keep the lower edge of the folded section aligned with the base. Wrap the ribbon around the center.

12. Secure as before. Turn the center upside down. Take several stitches through the base to secure. End off the thread.

13. Completed center.

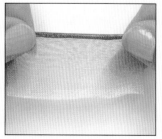

14. Petals. On one piece of ribbon, roll the top edge down for two tight rolls.

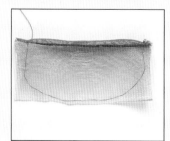

15. Handstitch running stitches in a 'U' shape from rolled edge, down, across the bottom and back up.

16. Pull up the running stitches to gather and tie off so the petal 'cups'. Repeat for the remaining petals.

17. Securing the petals. Cup one petal around the center. Align the gathering on the petal with the stitching through the center.

18. Stitch with tiny stitches to secure.

19. Attach the remaining petals in the same manner, ensuring that they slightly overlap the previous petals.

20. Trim excess ribbon at the base. **Completed rose.**

CONTINUOUS PETAL FLOWER

The large flower is made from a 17.5cm (6 ⅞") length of ribbon.
For the two smaller flowers cut a 12.5cm (4 ⅞") length of ribbon for each flower.
For photographic purposes we used contrasting beads and thread.

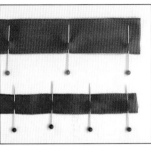

1. Leaving 7mm (⁵⁄₁₆") at both ends, mark ribbon for the larger flower at 4cm (1 ½") intervals. Mark smaller flower at 2.5cm (1") intervals.

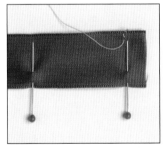  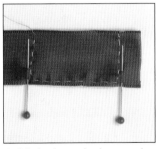 

2. Beginning 7mm (⁵⁄₁₆") from the right hand end, anchor the thread at the top edge with two tiny back stitches.

3. Using tiny running stitches, stitch across the ribbon to the opposite side.

4. Stitch along the lower edge of the ribbon almost to the next mark. Turn and stitch back to the top edge.

5. Take one stitch over the top edge of the ribbon. Following steps 3 and 4, continue until reaching the end of the ribbon.

6. Hold the ribbon firmly in the left hand. Tightly pull up the running stitches to gather the four petals. Do not allow the ribbon to twist.

7. Using the same thread, sew the ends and then the base of each petal together, working them into a circle. End off the thread.

8. Center of large flower. Using doubled thread, stitch a bead over the center to conceal the edges.

9. Center of small flower. Stitch a cluster of seed beads over the center to conceal the edges.

SILKEN TOUCH

A cluster of irresistible strawberries, each saying "I love you".
Annie Humphris of South Australia has designed a perfect present
for the Mother who has everything.

REQUIREMENTS

Fabric

15cm x 88cm wide (6" x 35") piece of
pale pink silk dupioni

15cm x 22cm wide (6" x 9") piece of
pale blue silk dupioni

Threads, Ribbons, Beads & Needles

See page 29.

Supplies

Small amount of fiber-fill

Sharp HB pencil

THIS DESIGN USES

Back stitch · Beading · Blanket stitch
Bullion knot · Detached chain · Fly stitch
French knot · Rolled ribbon rose · Straight stitch

PREPARATION FOR EMBROIDERY

See the liftout sheet for the embroidery designs.

Transferring the design

Place the piece of silk fabric over the corresponding
embroidery design in the liftout sheet,
aligning the placement marks on the
design with the straight grain of the
fabric. Using the pencil, trace the outline
of the strawberry and the design.

EMBROIDERY

All embroidery is worked before
cutting out the strawberry shape,
except for attaching the crystal
beads, the rolled roses and tiny beads
over the seam. These are
attached after the seam has
been stitched and before
inserting the filling.

ORDER OF WORK

Crystal strawberry

Embroider a group of four detached chain leaves with the green thread at the marked positions for the tiny beaded design *(diag 1)*.

Diag 1

Diag 2

Stitch four tiny beads over each group of green leaves *(diag 2)*.

Using the gold thread, work a pair of detached chain leaves at each marked position. Add a French knot with two straight stitches at the top of each pair of leaves *(diag 3)*.

Before inserting the filling attach a crystal to each pair of gold leaves, just below the French knot. Add a crystal to the tip of the strawberry.

Diag 3

Rose strawberry

Make seven rolled ribbon roses.

Embroider four to five detached chain leaves of varying sizes at the marked positions.

After stitching the seam, embroider any remaining leaves and attach the roses at the junctions of the leaves.

Using three strands each of D and F, stitch a small tassel at the tip of the strawberry with three to four loops 2.5cm (1") in length. Trim the ends of the tassel.

Using one strand of F, wrap the thread around the top of the tassel. This will form a base for attaching the two circles of beads (approximately sixteen beads).

Rosebud strawberry

Work the bullion rosebuds, then the detached chain and French knot foliage. Attach the groups of three tiny beads.

After the strawberry has been constructed, work the tassel at the tip in the same manner as before. Attach the circle of beads just above the tassel (approximately five beads).

Pansy strawberries

Embroider each pair of pansies in blanket stitch. Work five to six small straight stitches, radiating from the center, over the petals for highlights.

Work a French knot in the center of each pansy and a fly stitch outlining each of the two top petals.

Work the stems and leaves next, followed by the gold highlighting stitches, finishing each one with a French knot.

Complete any embroidery over the seam. Work the tassel in the same manner as before. Attach a circle of six to seven beads just above the tassel.

CONSTRUCTION

See pages 113 - 114.

~ THREADS, RIBBONS, BEADS & NEEDLES ~

Anchor stranded cotton
A = 100 vy dk lavender
B = 109 violet
C = 110 dk violet
D = 842 vy lt khaki green
E = 843 lt khaki green
F = 893 vy lt shell pink

Anchor Marlitt stranded rayon
G = 867 dk golden yellow
H = 895 lt khaki green

Edmar Glory rayon thread
I = 129 old gold

Au Papillon metallic thread
J = bright gold

YLI 601 fine metallic thread
K = gold

Hanah hand-dyed silk ribbon 25mm (1") wide
L = 2m (2yd 7") blushing bride
M = 1.2m (1yd 12") lavender rosebud

Glen Lorin 7mm ($^5/_{16}$") hand-dyed silk ribbon
N = 80cm (32") Annie's request

Czech 10mm x 6mm wide ($^3/_8$" x $^1/_4$") faceted teardrop crystal
O = pink (9 crystals)

Mill Hill antique beads
P = 03021 royal pearl
Q = 03051 misty
No. 9 sharp needle
No. 10 milliner's needle

All embroidery is worked with one strand unless otherwise specified.

Crystal strawberry

Crystal design

Foliage = J (detached chain French knot, straight stitch)

Crystals = O

Small cluster design

Leaves = D (detached chain)

Beads = Q

Rose strawberry

Rose = N
(rolled ribbon rose)

Leaves = D
(2 strands, detached chain)

Beads = Q

Tassel = D and F
(3 strands of each)

Rosebud strawberry

Rosebud = F (2 bullion knots, 12 - 14 wraps)

Foliage = D
(detached chain, French knot)

Beads = Q

Tassel = D and F
(3 strands of each)

Pansy strawberries

Upper petals = C
(2 strands
blanket stitch)
A (fly stitch)

Lower petals = B
(blanket stitch)

Center = I (French knot, 2 wraps)

Petal highlights = G
(straight stitch)

Stems = E (back stitch)

Leaves = H (detached chain)

Highlights = K (straight stitch French knot)

Beads = P

Tassel = A and C or E
(3 strands of each), K (6 strands)

MAKING THE TWISTED CORD

The twisted cord is used for the hanger of each strawberry.

The cords are made with two to four strands of each color.

We used a spinster to make our twisted cord.

Step 1. Cut three strands of each color measuring five times the finished length. Fold in half to give twelve strands.

Step 2. Knot the cut ends together and hook the loop of the folded end over a cup hook or door handle.

Step 3. Hook the knotted end onto the hook of the spinster.

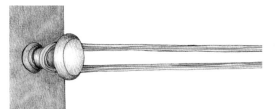

Step 4. Keeping threads taut, twist them in a clockwise direction until the twist has the desired tension.

Step 5. Fold the twisted threads in half, holding at the half way point. Ensure the threads are kept taut.

Step 6. Keeping twisted threads fully stretched, release 10cm - 15cm (4" - 6") at a time until all the cord is twisted.

Step 7. Remove the loop from the doorknob and knot the ends together. **Completed twisted cord.**

GLAD TIDINGS

by CAROLYN PEARCE of NEW SOUTH WALES

A romantic patchwork stocking with luscious embroidery and shimmering beads,
bestowing a simple grandeur to your mantle or tree.

THIS DESIGN USES

Back stitch · Beading · Blanket stitch
Bullion knot · Colonial knot
Colonial knot - running stitch
combination rose · Coral stitch
Couching · Detached chain
Fly stitch · French knot
Herringbone stitch · Running stitch
Stem stitch · Straight stitch
Zigzag chain stitch

REQUIREMENTS

Fabric

30cm (12") square of pale ivory
silk dupioni

20cm (8") square of ivory silk dupioni

20cm x 25cm wide (8" x 10") piece of
cream silk broadcloth

20cm (8") square of quilter's muslin

Supplies

20cm x 25cm (8" x 10") piece of thin
wadding

20cm x 18mm wide (8" x ¾") lace
insertion with bow design

1 x 4mm (³/₁₆") mother-of-pearl
shank button

2 x 4mm (³/₁₆") mother-of-pearl buttons

20cm (8") gold gilt millary wire

6mm wide (¼") Tiger tape

Invisible thread

White Nymo thread

Threads, Beads, Ribbons & Needles

See page 33.

PREPARATION FOR EMBROIDERY

See the liftout pattern for the stocking template.

Preparing the patchwork front

Trace the stocking template and design lines onto the muslin. Following the cutting layouts, trace the patchwork shapes onto the pale ivory and ivory dupioni and cut out.

"The patches do not have to be on the straight grain of the fabric - they are more interesting if they are not." ~ CAROLYN

Matching marks, attach the pieces to the muslin shape, matching the numerical sequence *(diag 1)*.

Work all the embroidery just past the stitchline.

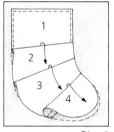

Diag 1

Beading near this line will be completed after the stocking has been stitched together.

Transferring the design

Rows for embroidery

Place the tracing paper over the template in the liftout sheet. Using the pencil, trace the markings for the lace placement, rows of embroidery and the front embroidery designs.

Tape the tracing to a window or a light box. With the right side facing, place the prepared silk dupioni over the tracing, aligning placement marks. Using the pencil, trace the embroidery designs.

Embroidery designs on back and lining

Trace the appropriate initial and date onto tracing paper. With the right side of the stocking back facing up, place it over the tracing, aligning placement marks with the straight grain of the fabric. Trace the initial and date.

Trace the spray on the broadcloth lining in the same manner.

EMBROIDERY

Use the between needle when working with the metallic threads and the milliner's needle when stitching the bullion knots. The chenille needle is used for all ribbon work and for making the tassels.

Center the lace over the join of the two top pieces, pin and machine stitch in place.

Order of work

Row 1

Embroider groups of five blanket stitches into the same hole in the fabric at the top of the stitches, 5mm (³/₁₆") above the lace. Attach one bead (M) to the tip of each group. Work three detached chain stitches above the bead.

Work a straight stitch stem between each blanket stitch group. Add two detached chain leaves and work the flowers with six bead petals (K) and a gold bead center (L).

Row 2 (lace)

With one strand of F, weave in and out of the holes in the lace to outline the bows. Work a colonial knot in the center of each bow. Stitch three tiny beaded flowers at the top of each bow. This creates a wavy effect, as alternate bows are upside down. Form each flower in the same manner as the flowers in row 1. Surround with four pairs of tiny detached chain leaves. Attach one bead (M) on the lace dot between each bow. Using F, embroider two detached chain leaves above the bead and three straight stitches below the bead.

Row 3

Turn the fabric sideways to work a row of zigzag chain stitch below the lace for leaves. Turn the fabric back to the previous position. Work one straight stitch in D in the center of a pair of leaves and one on each side using H. Add three gold beads at the tips.

Row 4

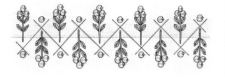

Lay a foundation of herringbone stitch in F, working the stitches between the guidelines.

Work a straight stitch at each intersection with G. Using D, work two pairs of detached chain leaves to each straight stitch. Attach three beads (M) to each stem and one bead (L) on the opposite side of the intersection.

Row 5

Turn the fabric upside down. Using E, work the crests with five blanket stitches and the troughs with stem stitch *(diag 2)*.

Diag 2

Near the tip of the three central blanket stitches and at the base of the other two, work a pair of detached chain leaves in H. Add bead flowers to the center stems with K and L and one bead (M) to the end stems *(diag 3)*.

Diag 3

With the fabric still upside down, work a detached chain in F and add three smaller detached chains at the tip in D. Couch a straight stitch on each side and add three gold beads to the tip of each *(diag 4)*.

Diag 4

Work three straight stitches and two detached chains above the row of stem stitch in H. Attach a bead (M) to the tip of each straight stitch.

Below the curve, work five detached chain stitches in H *(diag 5)*.

Diag 5

Bow and rose spray

Tie a bow with the satin ribbon and pin in place at the marked position on the stocking front. Referring to the photograph, arrange the tails on the fabric. Pin at each fold. Couch the loops and tails in place with colonial knots. Attach the buttons with one strand of A. Attach each tiny heart with a gold bead.

Work five colonial knot-running stitch combination roses above the bow.

Embroider three rosebuds above the ribbon roses and one pair of rosebuds on each side.

Work two tiny straight stitches at the tip of each bud and a fly stitch with a long anchoring stitch around the base. Stitch detached chain leaves among the buds.

Work a pair of fly stitch leaves on each side of the spray and one leaf near the tip of each bow loop.

Attach the butterfly with the invisible thread by working the stitches parallel to its body.

Fan and rose spray

Fan

Work eleven blanket stitches in E for the ribs of the fan. Just below the upper edge, work a row of coral stitch in H. Between each rib, and starting at the row of coral stitch, work a straight stitch in H. At the upper edge, couch a row of E to form scallops and then add five evenly spaced French knots just under each peak. Attach a gold bead above each peak. Work a colonial knot between each rib of the blanket stitch and the edge.

Rose spray

Embroider a bullion rose at the lower tip of the fan. Add three pairs of rosebuds in the same manner as the rosebuds at the top of the design. Stitch detached chain leaves around the roses and buds.

Form the bow and couch in place.

Initial on back

Baste the wadding to the wrong side of the stocking back. Work stem stitch around the outline of the initial and embroider a rose spray in a similar manner to the roses on the front. Attach gold beads to the wide section of the initial. Work the date in tiny back stitches.

Embroider the roses and rosebuds in the same manner as on the front of the stocking.

Rosebuds on lining

Embroider these in the same manner as on the front of the stocking.

CONSTRUCTION

See pages 114 - 116.

~ THREADS, RIBBONS, BEADS & NEEDLES ~

Threads

Anchor stranded cotton
A = 880 dk sand

Madeira stranded silk
B = 1910 lt mushroom

Madeira metallic thread no. 40
C = 6 gold

Au Ver à Soie Metallics Antique
D = 222 lt gold

Au Ver à Soie Metallics Bourdon
E = 1102 lt gold

F = 3002 gold
G = 6012 dk gold

YLI metallic thread
H = 7 pale green

Colour Streams 4mm (³/₁₆") wide silk ribbon
J = 50cm (20") antique ivory

Beads

Mill Hill petite beads
K = 40123 cream
L = 40557 old gold

Mill Hill antique beads
M = 03050 champagne ice

Mill Hill glass treasures
N = 12126 butterfly
O = 12234 heart (2)

Satin ribbon 3mm (¹/₈") wide
P = 25cm (10") cream

Needles

No. 9 between
No. 11 milliner's
No. 22 chenille

~ EMBROIDERY KEY ~

All embroidery is worked with one strand unless otherwise specified.

Bow and rose spray

Bow = P (tied bow), A
(2 strands, colonial knot)

Roses = J (colonial knot-running stitch combination rose)

Rosebuds = B (2 bullion knots, 8-10 wraps)
H (straight stitch, fly stitch)

Foliage = H (detached chain, fly stitch)

Row 1

Top edge = E (blanket stitch)
M (beading), D (detached chain)

Stem = G (straight stitch)

Leaves = H (detached chain)

Flowers = K and L (beading)

Row 2 (lace)

Bow = F (weaving, colonial knot)
G (straight stitch)

Flowers = K and L (beading)
G (detached chain)

Tiny flowers = M (beading)
F (detached chain, straight stitch)

Row 3

Leaves = F (zigzag chain), H (straight stitch)

Stem = D (straight stitch)

Flower = L (beading)

Row 4

Foundation = F (herringbone stitch)

Stem = G (straight stitch)

Leaf = D (detached chain)

Flower = M (beading)

Single beads = L (beading)

Row 5

Crest of scallop = E (blanket stitch)

Flowers on crest = K and L (beading)

Bud = M (beading)

Leaves = H (detached chain)

Flowers below crest = D and F
(detached chain), F (straight stitch couching), L (beading)

Trough = E (stem stitch)

Flowers in trough = H (straight stitch detached chain), M (beading)

Leaves = H (detached chain)

Fan and rose spray

Fan

Ribs = E (blanket stitch)
H (coral stitch, straight stitch)

Upper edge of fan = E (couching)
G (French knot), L (beading)

Rose spray

Center = B (2 bullion knots, 8 wraps)

Inner petals = B
(3 bullion knots, 10 wraps)

Outer petals = B
(2 bullion knots, 12 wraps)

Rosebuds = B
(2 bullion knots, 8 - 10 wraps)

Foliage = H (straight stitch fly stitch, detached chain)

Bow = G (detached chain, couching)

Initial and date on back

Initial = E (stem stitch), L (beading)

Date = E (back stitch)

Roses

Center = B (2 bullion knots, 8 wraps)

Inner petals = B
(3 bullion knots, 10 wraps)

Outer petals = B
(2 bullion knots, 12 wraps)

Rosebuds

Petals = B
(2 bullion knots, 8 - 10 wraps)

Foliage = H (straight stitch fly stitch, detached chain)

Rosebuds on lining

Petals = B (2 bullion knots 8 - 10 wraps)

Foliage = H (straight stitch, fly stitch couching, detached chain)

ANTIQUE GOLD

by LIZ VICKERY of SOUTH AUSTRALIA

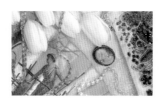

Functional, fashionable and frivolous, handbags are part of a woman's identity. This exquisite bag mirrors the Dorothy-style shape of the early 1900's and reflects the love of all things bright and glittery.

REQUIREMENTS

Fabric

30cm x 45cm wide (12" x 18") piece of cream moiré fabric

30cm (12") square of cream silk dupioni for the lining

Beads, Thread & Needle

See page 36.

Supplies

Beige beading thread

Black beading thread

20cm x 8cm wide (8" x 3 ¼") hand dyed lace motif

15cm x 7cm wide (6" x 2 ¾") hand dyed lace motif

7 x 10mm (³⁄₈") wide small tea-dyed lace flowers

30cm (12") square of thin wadding eg Pellon

Small amount of polyester fiber-fill

10.5cm (4 ⅛") wide gold frame (measured hinge to hinge)

1.25m (1yd 13 ¼") gold plaited braid

80cm x 4mm wide (31 ½" x ³⁄₁₆") gold braid

80cm x 3mm wide (31 ½" x ⅛") gold cord

2 x 8mm (¼") gold split rings

25cm (10") embroidery hoop

THIS DESIGN USES

Beading · Fly stitch · Straight stitch

PREPARATION FOR EMBROIDERY

See the liftout sheet for the pattern and embroidery guide.

Preparing the fabric

Cut a 30cm (12") square from the moiré fabric. To prevent the fabric from fraying while working the beading and embroidery, stitch around all edges with a machine zigzag or overlock stitch.

EMBROIDERY

See pages 38 and 39 for step-by-step instructions for beading, working with lengths of beads and beading a leaf.

All beading and embroidery is worked with the fabric in the hoop.

"I used several lace motifs to create my design. Sections of a smaller piece were added to a larger motif. I then placed seven small lace flowers around and over the design." ~ LIZ

Front of bag

Carefully cut the lace motifs and arrange on the right side of the moiré to give the desired effect.

Referring to the pattern and embroidery guide, center the front piece over the pattern and pin the motifs in place. Trace the pattern outline.

Using machine sewing thread to match the lace, attach with small hand stitches. Refer to the embroidery key and photographs as you work for the placement of the beads.

Bead the large flower first, following the design lines. Slightly pad the petal pocket with a tiny amount of fiber-fill. Catch the lip of the petal with tiny stitches as you embellish it with beads.

Work the bow next, creating strands of beads and couching them into position. Follow the design lines of the lace as you work the beading.

Embellish the leaves following the step-by-step instructions on page 39.

Fill in the smaller flowers with clusters of beads. Embroider the gold fly stitch branches. Decorate around the design, creating groups of small bead flowers. Work gold fly stitches on the motif and stitch tiny groups of beads over any remaining areas.

BEADS, THREADS & NEEDLES

Czech size 11 glass seed beads

A = 558-C iris, brown (1 string)

Maria George size 11 beads

B = 7015 frosted lilac

C = 9102 plum

D = 9126 army green

Maria George Delica beads

E = DBR 23 lt bronze iris

F = DBR 123 olive gray

G = DBR 371 olive green

H = DBR 863 shark gray

I = DBR 865 dk chocolate

Maria George Delica hex cut beads

J = DBC 501 gold iris

8mm (³/₈") glass crystal beads

K = lt amethyst (11 beads)

4mm (³/₁₆") glass rondels

L = lt amethyst (23 beads)

M = dk amethyst (17 beads)

Czech 4mm (³/₁₆") glass beads

N = lt amethyst (10 beads)

O = dk amethyst (13 beads)

Czech AB coated 4mm (³/₁₆") glass beads

P = lt amethyst (4 beads)

Q = dk amethyst (71 beads)

Mill Hill antique frosted glass beads

R = 62056 boysenberry

DMC stranded metallic thread

S = 5282 gold

No. 10 milliner's needle

EMBROIDERY KEY

All embroidery is worked with one strand unless otherwise specified.

Large flower

Top petal = C, E, N, O, Q and R (beading)

Petals = B, E and R (beading)

Raised center = A (beading)
S (fly stitch, straight stitch)

Small bead flowers

Petals = A (beading)

Center = C (beading)

Large leaves

Center vein = D (beading)

Sides of leaf = F and G (beading)

Small leaves = E, F, G and J (beading), S (fly stitch)

Flower motifs = C, L, M, N, O, P, Q and R (beading)

Bow = F, G, H and I (beading)

Scattered flowers = H and I (beading), S (fly stitch, straight stitch)

Scattered leaves = B and F (beading) S (fly stitch, straight stitch)

Fringe = B, C, E, K and Q (beading)

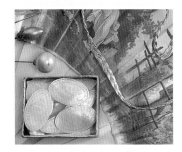

CONSTRUCTION

See pages 116 and 117.

FINISHING

The beaded fringe is worked after the bag has been constructed. There are eleven long tassels, each loop overlapping the next.

Each tassel is made up by threading beads in the following order:

10 x E, 1 x B, 1 x Q, 1 x B

10 x E, 1 x B, 1 x Q, 1 x C, 1 x K

1 x C, 1 x Q, 1 x B, 10 x E, 1 x B

1 x Q, 1 x B, 10 x E

Secure the beading thread with back stitches at the lower left corner of the bag. Work from left to right. Thread the beads onto the thread following the bead sequence for each loop. Stitch onto the fabric with back stitches placing the first and last bead of each loop approximately 15mm (⁵⁄₈") apart. For the next loop, overlap the previous loop starting 7.5mm (⁷⁄₁₆") from the beginning of the first *(diag 1)*. Continue in this manner to the right hand corner.

Diag 1

Hints on Beading

1. Use short lengths of thread. A long thread is more likely to tangle or knot and will eventually fray during use.

2. Always finish off securely. Take the thread to the back of the fabric and work several back stitches before trimming.

3. Use a long, thin needle as some beads have very small holes. Milliner's and beading needles are most suitable.

4. Always work with the fabric in a hoop so it is easier to maintain an even tension on the thread.

5. Use stitches that are exactly the same length as the bead. A stitch that is too long will allow the bead to move and one that is too short will prevent the bead from lying securely against the fabric.

BEADS AND BAGS

Early in the 1800's, the first small bags developed in response to changing fashions.

As garments became much more slender, flimsy and close fitting, there was no longer room to conceal pockets, which were then separate garments made of plain washable cotton. These pockets were attached to tapes tied around the waist and were reached through slashes in the sides of skirts. Pockets were later inserted in the lining of garments but the fashion for bags had begun and was unstoppable.

Delicate bags were at first used to carry dance cards, diaries, fans, visiting

cards and most importantly, fine linen handkerchiefs.

Such bags became known as 'indispensables' in Britain and 'ridicules' in France. As the 19th century progressed, the term 'ridicule' evolved into 'reticule', a term that was used in both French and English.

The term 'handbag' first referred to large leather bags attached to a metal or wooden frame. As the leather bag became more widely used, the term gradually referred to many styles of bags.

The terms 'purse' and 'change purse' also became popular and by the early 1900's the bag became the perfect finishing touch to any outfit.

Bags soon reflected the moods of fashion, from the languid 1800's look to

the tailored style as the centuries progressed.

They became more exotic during the rage for the Orient that swept Europe early in the 20th century and then more restrained after the onset of World War I.

With the rise of the use of cigarettes and cosmetics and the modern woman of the 1920's who dared to smoke and powder her nose in public, came the larger shape of the handbag.

Despite all these changes, a woman's handbag has always been an essential accessory.

BEADING

There are many ways of attaching beads to fabric,
from a simple back stitch, couching or running stitch,
to using a tambour hook and frame.
The secure method, used here, is back stitch.

We used contrasting thread and beads for
photographic purposes.

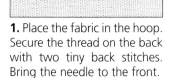

1. Place the fabric in the hoop.
Secure the thread on the back
with two tiny back stitches.
Bring the needle to the front.

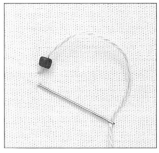

2. Place a bead onto the
needle and slide it down to
the fabric. Take a stitch the
same length as the bead.

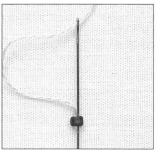

3. Pull the needle to the back
and secure with a back stitch.
Bring the thread through and
take the needle back through
the bead.

4. Pull the thread through.
Place a second bead onto the
needle and slide it down to
the fabric.

5. Secure the bead in the
same manner as before.

WORKING WITH LENGTHS OF BEADS

Attaching a length of beads, sometimes called
Lazy Squaw Stitch, was first developed by the American
Indians. It is a very quick way to attach a string of beads.

We used contrasting thread and beads for
photographic purposes.

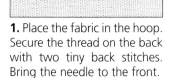

1. Place the fabric in the hoop.
Secure the thread on the back
with two tiny back stitches.
Bring the needle to the front.

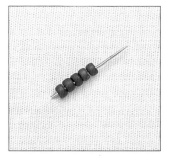

2. Thread 5 - 9 beads (or the
required number) onto the
needle.

3. Take the needle to the back
allowing the beads to sit flat.
Repass the needle back
through the beads. Secure
with two back stitches.

4. To bead a curve, place beads
in position. Take the needle to
the back and secure. Couch
between the beads to hold in
the required position.

5. Take the needle to the back
and finish off as before.

BEADING A LEAF

The larger bead encrusted leaves are created from three different shades of beads.
We used contrasting beads and thread for photographic purposes.

1. Center vein. Bring the thread to the front at the base of the leaf. Thread enough beads onto the needle to cover the center vein.

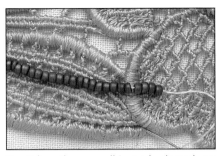

2. Take the needle and thread to the back at the tip, just inside the edge of the leaf.

3. Stitching from the tip towards the base, work a couching stitch after every second bead.

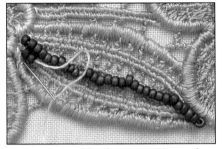

4. First side of leaf. Bring to the surface at the base of the leaf. Thread two beads and take the needle to the back, alongside the first rib.

5. Re-emerge close to center vein. Pull thread through. Thread on three beads and lay them diagonally towards outer edge. Take needle to the back.

6. Continue working, starting in a new segment of the lace each time.

7. Towards the end of the leaf, angle the last stitch until it is almost parallel with the center vein.

8. Second side of leaf. Re-emerge at the base. Pull the thread through. Thread on two beads and take to the back alongside the first rib.

9. Re-emerge in the next section. Pull the thread through. Thread on two beads, take the thread to the back just inside the edge of the leaf.

10. Continue working, filling each segment with two beads.

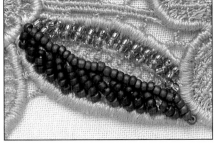

11. Second row. Re-emerge at base. Pull thread through. Thread on two beads and take to the back between the beads of the previous row.

12. Continue working along leaf, ensuring end of each beaded stitch is placed between sections of previous row. **Completed beaded leaf.**

● ● ●

BERRY DELIGHT

*The texture and tantalising
warmth of Jan Kerton's
stumpwork berries is so lifelike
it makes you want to reach out
and touch them.
Delicious strawberries,
blackberries, mulberries and
currants decorate the lids of
the little trinket boxes.*

Clusters of miniature stumpwork berries decorate the lids of four trinket pots. Beads and felt have been cleverly incorporated into the embroidery to create each fruit.

REQUIREMENTS

Fabric

You will need the following amounts of fabric for each design

12.5cm (5") square of pale gold silk satin

12.5cm (5") square of cream homespun

Threads, Beads & Needles

See page 44.

Supplies

4 trinket pots with lid diameter of 4cm (1 ½")

6cm x 10cm wide (2 ⅜" x 4") piece of red felt

Water-soluble stabilizer

01 brown Micron Pigma permanent marking pen

10cm (4") embroidery hoop

Small amount of fiber-fill

PREPARATION FOR EMBROIDERY

See the liftout sheet for the embroidery designs.

We recommend you bind each ring of the hoop with cotton tape or bias binding ironed flat.

Transferring the design

Center the homespun over your chosen design, aligning the placement marks with the straight grain of the fabric and tape in place. Using the pen, trace the design.

EMBROIDERY

See the step-by-step instructions on pages 45 - 47 for making the strawberry, blueberry, large blackberry, small blackberry, mulberry and red currant.

See the liftout sheet for the strawberry templates.

All embroidery is worked with the fabric in the hoop.

Use the no. 26 tapestry needle for the whipping and the no. 9 crewel needle for all remaining embroidery.

With wrong sides together, place the piece of silk over the homespun.

Working from the wrong side, join the two layers together with tiny running stitches around the circle.

THESE DESIGNS USE

Beading · Blanket stitch

Detached chain · Holbein stitch

Long and short stitch

Needlewoven picot · Pistil stitch

Running stitch · Straight stitch

Tufting · Whipping · Wrapping

DESIGN 1

DESIGN 2

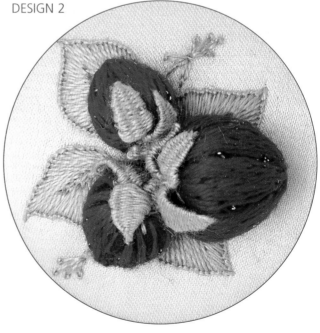

THE FINISHED LID MEASURES 4CM (1½").

Design 1

Order of work

Stems

Stitching from the back, work the stems in Holbein stitch.

Using the same thread, whip the stitches on the right side.

Small leaves

Stitching from the back of the work, embroider a tiny straight stitch for the center of each leaf.

On the right side of the work, stitch a detached chain around each straight stitch.

Large leaves

Stitching from the back of the work, embroider the outline and vein of each leaf in Holbein stitch.

On the right side of the work, whip the vein of the leaf.

Starting at the base, work blanket stitch along one half of the leaf, angling the stitches near the tip. Work a small anchoring stitch at the tip. Work the second half of the leaf in the same manner.

Berries

Make one small strawberry, one large and one small blackberry, two mulberries, two red currants and two blueberries following step-by-step instructions on pages 45 to 47.

Design 2

Order of work

Stem

Work the stem in the same manner as design 1.

Strawberry flowers

At each end of the stem work a pair of detached chain leaves. Noting the color change, embroider four tiny pistil stitches close to the leaves of the spent flowers.

Large leaves

Embroider the leaves in the same manner as the large leaves in design 1.

Berries

Make one large and two small strawberries following the step-by-step instructions on page 45.

Design 3

Order of work

Stems

Work the stems in the same manner as design 1.

Leaves

Work the leaves in the same manner as the small leaves in design 1.

Berries

Make two small blackberries, three red currants and three blueberries following the step-by-step instructions on pages 46 and 47.

After the berries have been attached, add the single beads at the positions indicated on the pattern.

Design 4

Order of work

Leaves

Working from the back, embroider a straight stitch for each leaf.

On the right side of the work stitch a detached chain over each straight stitch.

Berries

Make one large and one small blackberry, one mulberry, three red currants and three blue-berries following the step-by-step instructions on pages 46 and 47.

CONSTRUCTION

See page 117.

DESIGN 3

DESIGN 4

THREADS, BEADS & NEEDLES

From the list below, select the requirements for your chosen design.

Design 1

A, B, C, D, E, G, H, I, J, K, L, M N, O, P, Q and R

Design 2

B, E, F, G and H

Design 3

A, C, E, G, I, J, K, L, M, O, P and Q

Design 4

A, B, C, D, G, I, J, K, L, M, N, O P, Q and R

Presencia stranded cotton

A = 0007 black

B = 1906 garnet

C = 3327 French navy

D = 5151 fern green

E = 5224 lt khaki green

F = 8017 lt mocha

G = 9275 variegated red plum

Kreinik blending filament

H = 205C antique gold

Mill Hill glass seed beads

I = 00367 garnet

J = 02014 black

Mill Hill antique glass beads

K = 03024 mocha

Mill Hill frosted glass beads

L = 60367 garnet

M = 62014 black

N = 62032 cranberry

O = 62056 boysenberry

Mill Hill glass pebble beads

P = 05025 ruby

Q = 05081 black frost

Mill Hill small glass bugle beads

R = 72012 royal plum

Needles

No. 9 crewel

No. 26 tapestry

EMBROIDERY KEY

All embroidery is worked with one strand unless otherwise specified.

Design 1

Stems and small leaves

Stems = D
(whipped Holbein stitch)

Small leaves = D
(straight stitch, detached chain)

Large leaves

Outline = D (Holbein stitch)

Vein = D (whipped Holbein stitch)

Leaf = D (blanket stitch)

Strawberry = B and G
(2 strands, long and short stitch)

Seeds = H
(2 strands, straight stitch)

Sepal = E (needlewoven picot)

Blackberries

Large blackberry = A and P
(wrapping), A, J, L, M and N
(beading)

Small blackberry = A, J and M
(beading)

Mulberries = B and R (wrapping)
B, I, L and O (beading)

Red currants = G and P (wrapping)

Top = G and K (beading)

Blueberries = C and Q (wrapping)

Top = C (2 strands, tufting)

Design 2

Stem = E
(whipped Holbein stitch)

Strawberry flowers

Small leaves = E
(detached chain)

Flowers = F (pistil stitch)

Large leaves

Outline = E (Holbein stitch)

Vein = E
(whipped Holbein stitch)

Leaf = E (blanket stitch)

Strawberries = B and G
(2 strands, long and short stitch)

Seeds = H
(2 strands, straight stitch)

Sepals = E (needlewoven picot)

Design 3

Stems and leaves

Stems = E
(whipped Holbein stitch)

Leaves = E
(straight stitch, detached chain)

Small blackberries = A, I, J, L
and M (beading)

Red currants = G and P (wrapping)

Top = G and K (beading)

Blueberries = C and Q (wrapping)

Top = C (2 strands, tufting)

Tiny scattered beads = G, I
and O (beading)

Design 4

Leaves = D (2 strands, straight
stitch, detached chain)

Blackberries

Large blackberry = A and P
(wrapping), A, J, L, M and N
(beading)

Small blackberry = A, J and L
(beading)

Mulberry = B and R (wrapping),
B, I, L and O (beading)

Red currants = G and P
(wrapping)

Top = G and K (beading)

Blueberries = C and Q (wrapping)

Top = C (2 strands, tufting)

MAKING A STRAWBERRY

● ● ●

When working with the variegated thread G, use only the red sections. The large and small strawberries are made in the same manner using the appropriate template.

1. Strawberry. Using the template, cut out the shape in felt.

2. Fold the felt in half to form a cone. Using a single strand of B, stitch the seam.

3. Using the same thread, work a gathering stitch around the opening. Pack firmly with fiber-fill.

4. Pull the gathering thread very firmly and stitch to close.

5. Starting at the tip using B and G, work long and short stitch, covering the felt shape.

6. Using H, work tiny vertical straight stitches randomly over the strawberry for seeds.

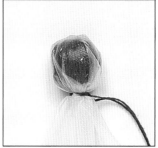

7. Sepals. Wrap the strawberry in the stabilizer and tie at the tip, so that it forms a handle.

8. Mark a spot at the center of the base, A. Place a pin into the side of the strawberry where the tip of the picot will be.

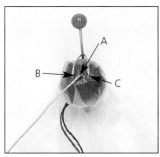

9. Bring needle up at B, approx 2-3mm (⅛") from A. Loop the thread behind the pin and take to the back at C. Emerge at A.

10. Take the thread clockwise around the pin.

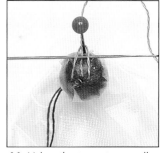

11. Using the tapestry needle, begin weaving under, over and under the base threads.

12. Continue weaving until the base threads are covered, packing them very firmly.

13. Take the needle to the back close to C and emerge close to A. Remove the pin.

14. Work 2 more sepals in the same manner around A. Tear away the stabilizer.

15. Using one strand of B, attach strawberry to fabric with small stab stitches. **Completed strawberry.**

MAKING A LARGE BLACKBERRY

1. Cut a 1m (40") length of A. Using the tapestry needle and leaving a 15cm (6") tail, thread the other end through Q.

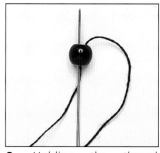

2. Holding the thread securely, take the needle and thread up through the bead, wrapping the bead firmly.

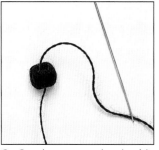

3. Continue wrapping in this manner, until the bead is completely covered.

4. Take the needle back through the bead catching some inside threads as the needle passes through. Tie ends together firmly. Do not cut off the thread.

5. Using the no. 9 crewel needle and a new thread, begin stitching the required small beads to the wrapped threads. Attach them one at a time.

6. Continue until threads are covered. To attach, take tails through fabric to the back and secure. **Completed large blackberry.**

MAKING A BLUEBERRY

1. Using C and Q, work the blueberry in the same manner as the red currant, omitting the seed bead on the top.

2. Once covered, take the thread back through the bead. Tie the ends together firmly. Do not cut off the tails.

3. Using 2 strands of C, take the thread down through the top of the berry, leaving a short tail.

4. Anchor the threads at the base of the blueberry, through the knot.

5. Take the needle back up through to the top of the blueberry and leave a short tail.

6. Trim the threads to 4mm (³/₁₆"). Brush them until they are fluffy. Attach as for the red currant. **Completed blueberry.**

MAKING A SMALL BLACKBERRY

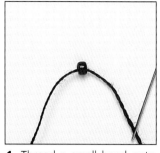

1. Thread a small bead onto the needle, leaving a tail of approximately 10cm (4").

2. Thread a second bead and pass the thread back through the first bead.

3. Thread five to fifteen more beads, one at a time, in the same manner.

4. Stitch through the beads, pulling the thread firmly forming a tight cluster.

5. Attach in the same manner as the large blackberry. **Completed small blackberry.**

MAKING A MULBERRY

1. Using a 1m (40") length of B and the no. 9 crewel needle, thread a bugle bead, R, onto the needle.

2. Wrap the bugle bead in the same manner as the blackberry with 4 - 6 wraps.

3. Tie the ends together securely. Do not cut. With new thread, attach the beads in the same manner as the large blackberry.

4. To attach, take the tails of thread through to the back of the fabric and secure. **Completed mulberry.**

MAKING A RED CURRANT

1. Follow steps 1 - 3 of the large blackberry to cover the large bead, P.

2. Thread small bead, K, onto needle. Take thread back through large bead. Secure at the base. Repeat.

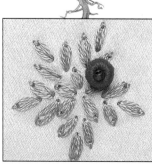

3. To attach, take tails of thread through to back of the fabric and secure. **Completed red currant.**

VEIL OF GOLD

by CHRISTINE BISHOP of SOUTH AUSTRALIA

Exquisite precision and luxurious materials combine to create this superb framed embroidery, reminiscent of an exotic jewelled lattice. The clever use of gold, pearls and red crystals creates the grand illusion of opulent beauty.

REQUIREMENTS

Fabric

50cm x 40cm wide (19 ¾" x 15 ¾") Graziano 'Ricamo' linen

50cm x 40cm wide (19 ¾" x 15 ¾") quilter's muslin

Supplies

Gütermann 100% sewing cotton ecru and no. 893 gold

Bees wax

Goldwork scissors

Stretcher frame or slate frame

Velvet cutting board

Tracing paper

Fine lead pencil

Threads & Needles

See page 50.

PREPARATION FOR EMBROIDERY

See the liftout pattern for the embroidery design.

See page 51 for step-by-step instructions for dressing a slate frame.

Transferring the design

Using the pencil, trace the design and placement marks onto the tracing paper.

THIS DESIGN USES

Beading · Couching

Tape the tracing to a window or light box. Center the muslin over the tracing, aligning the placement marks on the design with the straight grain of the fabric. Tape in place. The light shining through will make the design visible through the fabric. Trace the design onto the muslin. Place the linen on the untraced side of the muslin, aligning the straight grain of the fabrics. Mount the layered fabrics onto the frame following the step-by-step instructions. Tack through both layers of fabric, making the design visible on the right side.

EMBROIDERY

Use the gold sewing thread for couching the metal threads and the ecru sewing thread for attaching the beads and crystals.

Wax the threads before use to strengthen and prevent fraying.

Use the crewel needle for couching, the milliner's needle for sinking the gold twist and the beading needle for all beading.

Order of work

Cut a 1.7m (1yd 31") length of gold twist and fold it in half.

Beginning with the loop end of the doubled metal thread and starting in one corner of the design, couch the threads in place *(diag 1)*.

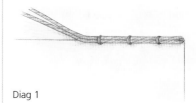

Diag 1

Space the couching stitches approximately 1cm (⅜") apart.

To turn the corner, couch the two threads separately *(diag 2)*.

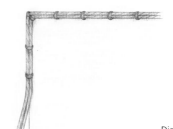

Diag 2

Continue in this manner until the border is complete.

THE FINISHED EMBROIDERY MEASURES 25CM X 17CM WIDE (10" X 6 ¾").

Sink the metal thread ends, one at a time, to the back of the work. Secure the ends behind the worked area and trim.

Cut appropriate lengths of gold twist to cover each diagonal line with doubled thread. Couch in place and secure in a similar manner as before.

At the intersections, take the threads over the top of previous couched lines.

Beading

Starting at the center of the design, attach a red crystal at the center of each intersection.

Stitch a large pearl in each of the right-angled corners of the lattice surrounding the crystal *(diag 3)*.

Diag 3

Bring the needle up close to the intersection and take a stitch long enough to accommodate the pearl *(diag 4)*.

Diag 4

Attach a large pearl at each right-angled corner along the outer edge and a second pearl directly opposite, outside the edge *(diag 5)*.

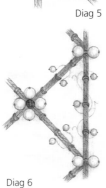

Diag 5

Attach small pearls at the marked positions of the outer edge and 'U' shaped scrolls *(diag 6)*.

Diag 6

At the four outer corners stitch three large pearls. Surround the central pearl with four small pearls *(diag 7)*.

Diag 7

Metal thread scrolls

Work with 30cm (12") lengths of the Japan gold to ensure it does not shred as it is pulled through the fabric.

Wrap the gold thread once around one pearl of a 'U' shape scroll. Couch it in place. Continue to couch the thread along the 'U' shape and wrap around the opposite pearl *(diag 8)*.

Diag 8

Bring the gold thread to the back of the work and carry to the next 'U' shape. Work all the 'U' shapes and scrolls in this manner.

Check purl embellishment

Cut the purl into 8mm (5/16") lengths. Cut the purl on a velvet board, made by covering a piece of cardboard with velvet. This will stop the purl from jumping around and assist in accurate cutting.

Diag 9

Thread a piece of purl onto the needle and attach around a large pearl *(diag 9)*.

Attach a piece of purl around all large pearls at the intersections and along the outer edge.

THREADS, BEADS & NEEDLES

Kreinik Japan no. 7

A = 002J gold

Benton and Johnson metal threads

B = 7m (7yd 24") dark gold 3 ply twist metal thread

C = 5gm no. 6 bright check purl

Beads

D = 210 x 4mm (3/16") pearls (10gm)

E = 280 x 2mm (1/16") pearls (10gm)

F = 40 x 3mm (1/8") red crystals

No. 1 milliner's needle

No. 9 crewel needle

No. 9 bead embroidery needle

❦ ❦ ❦

EMBROIDERY KEY

Outer edge = B (couching) C, D and E (beading)

Gold grid = B (couching) C, D, E and F (beading)

Scrolls = A (couching) E (beading)

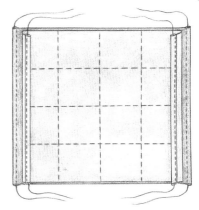

A slate frame keeps the fabric firm and on the straight grain at all times. The frame should be clamped to the work station to leave both hands free to handle the threads. The tension of the frame should be taut, not drum tight for metal thread, as this can result in puckering when the embroidery is removed from the frame.

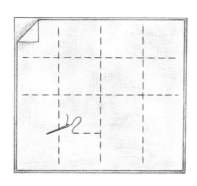

1. Baste the fabrics together beginning each row in the center, working to the sides in a grid.

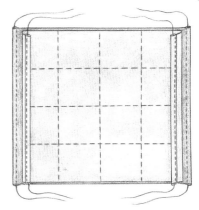

2. Fold a 1cm (³⁄₈") turning over a fine string on each side of each fabric and stitch, leaving 20cm (8") of string extending at each end.

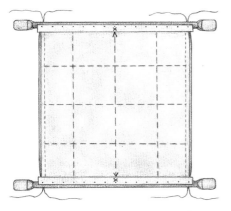

3. Mark the centers of the upper and lower edges and align with the center of the webbing on both rollers.

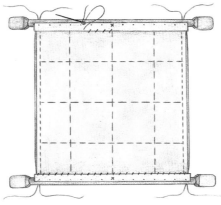

4. Work from the marked centers outwards to attach the fabrics to the webbing, using small overcast stitches.

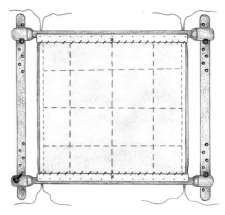

5. Roll surplus fabric onto a roller. Slot in the side pieces and peg to hold the fabrics firmly.

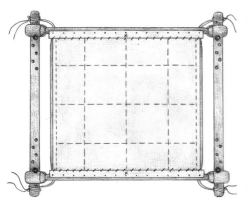

6. Tie off the eight ends of string tightly to the corners of the frame.

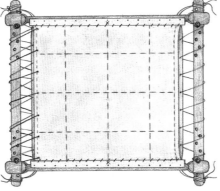

7. Using a large eyed needle, lace the sides of each fabric separately to the frame with string and tie the ends around the corners.

HANDLING CHECK PURL

Take care when handling this thread as it stretches easily like a fine spring.

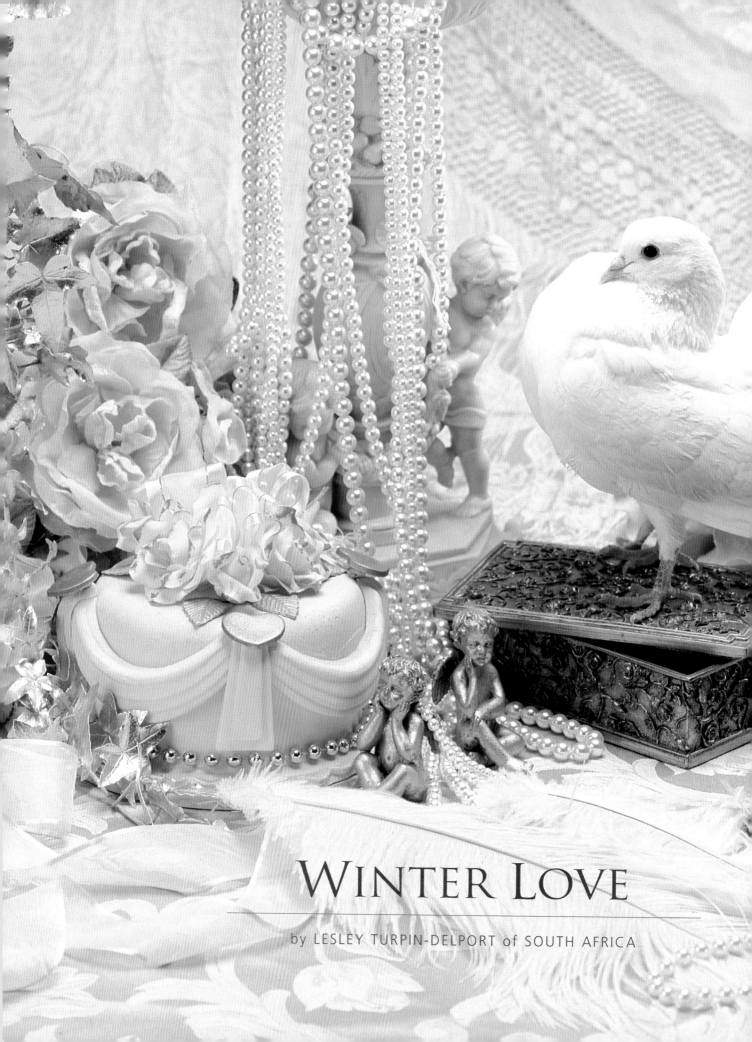

WINTER LOVE

by LESLEY TURPIN-DELPORT of SOUTH AFRICA

A sprig of luscious ripe blackberries arches gracefully across the center of this elegant ring cushion.
Threads and beads magically combine to create berries real enough to pick.
The rich hues of the fruit are echoed in the lustrous deep claret silk that forms a wide border.
Contrasting antique gold silk is used to create a piped edge and gold organza ribbons
provide the perfect place to tie the rings.

● ● ●

REQUIREMENTS

Fabric

25cm (10") square of off-white medium weight cotton

40cm (15 ¾") square of claret silk dupioni

40cm x 90cm wide (15 ¾" x 35 ½") piece of antique gold silk dupioni

40cm x 80cm wide (15 ¾" x 31 ½") piece of quilter's muslin

Supplies

10cm (4") square of appliqué paper

1.5m (1yd 23") of piping cord size 1

20cm (8") antique gold zip

Fiber-fill

15cm (6") embroidery hoop

Tracing paper

Fine black pen

Sharp green pencil

Threads, Beads, Ribbon & Needles

See page 56.

THIS DESIGN USES

Appliqué

Beading

Bullion knot

Detached blanket stitch bar

French knot

Long and short stitch

Long and short blanket stitch

Needlewoven bar

Overcast stitch

Pistil stitch

Stem stitch

PREPARATION FOR EMBROIDERY

See the liftout pattern for the embroidery design and leaf templates. See pages 117 and 118 for the cutting layouts.

Neaten the raw edges with a machine zigzag or overlock stitch to prevent fraying.

Transferring the design

Using the black pen, trace the design, placement marks and cutting lines onto the tracing paper. Tape the tracing to a window or light box. With the right side facing, center the off-white cotton over the tracing, aligning the placement marks with the straight grain of the fabric. Tape in place. The light shining through will make the design visible through the fabric.

Using the pencil, carefully trace the design onto the fabric.

"And the running blackberry, would adorn the parlor of heaven."

~ SONG OF MYSELF BY WALT WHITMAN ~

Preparing and attaching the appliqué pieces

Using the pen, trace the leaf templates onto the smooth side of the appliqué paper, allowing space between each tracing. Roughly cut around the shapes to separate the traced pieces.

Cut a 10cm (4") square from the piece of antique gold silk dupion referring to the cutting layout. Place the fabric right side down, onto a sheet of greaseproof paper. Place the appliqué paper pieces, rough side down, over the fabric. Fuse with a warm iron. Cut out the leaves along the marked outlines and peel off the paper backing. With the glue side facing the prepared cotton, place each leaf in position. Cover with baking paper and fuse.

EMBROIDERY

Refer to the embroidery key and close-up photograph for colour placement. Embroider the needlewoven bars and the spent flowers following the step-by-step instructions on pages 57 - 59.

Use the tapestry needle for the woven picots, the no. 10 crewel needle for the beading and the no. 9 crewel needle for all other embroidery. Use the chenille needle for attaching the ribbons.

Order of work

Leaves

Work the edge of the appliquéd leaves with long and short blanket stitch, enclosing the raw edge of the silk. Using light hazelnut, stitch the vein along the center of each leaf in stem stitch.

Outline the remaining leaf in stem stitch, using light fern green. Cover the leaf in long and short stitch. Stitch the center vein with verdigris.

Stems and stalks

Embroider a row of stem stitch along the main stem and cover with overcast stitch. Work the stalks of the berries and spent flowers with a long bullion knot for each, allowing them to arch slightly.

Spent flowers

Embroider the spent flowers following the step-by-step instructions.

Beaded blackberries

Referring to the photograph for colours, cover two blackberries marked

on the embroidery design with beads. Work a second layer of beads in the center of each berry to achieve a domed effect. Following the step-by-step instructions, embroider two or three needlewoven picots of varying lengths at the base of each berry for each calyx. Position the picots and couch the tip of each one in place.

Blackberries

Stitch the four remaining berries with closely packed French knots. Place two or three needlewoven bars at the base of each berry as before.

Ribbon bows

Thread a 35cm (13 ¾") length of ribbon into the chenille needle. Take a small stitch through the fabric at one of the marked positions. Tie a knot to keep the ribbon in place and trim the ends on the bias. Tie the ribbon into a neat bow. Repeat for the remaining ribbon.

CONSTRUCTION

See pages 117 - 119.

THE BLACKBERRY SYMBOLISES HEALING, MONEY AND PROTECTION.

THREADS, BEADS, RIBBON & NEEDLES

DMC stranded cotton

A = 221 vy dk shell pink

B = 371 verdigris

C = 422 lt hazelnut brown

D = 523 lt fern green

E = 524 vy lt fern green

F = 632 vy dk mocha

G = 840 med beige

H = 902 maroon

I = 938 ultra dk coffee brown

J = 3051 dk green-grey

K = 3354 lt dusky rose

L = 3772 dk mocha

Mill Hill glass seed beads

M = 00206 violet

N = 00367 garnet

O = 02013 red red

P = 02014 black

Mill Hill frosted glass beads

Q = 62032 cranberry

Mokuba no. 1500 organdy ribbon 7mm (⁵/₁₆") wide

R = 70cm (27 ½")
15 antique gold

Needles

No. 9 crewel

No. 10 crewel

No. 18 chenille

No. 22 tapestry

EMBROIDERY KEY

All embroidery is worked with one strand unless otherwise specified.

Leaves = B (appliqué, long and short blanket stitch), B or C (2 strands, stem stitch), B, C, E and L (long and short stitch)

Stems and stalks = D (2 strands stem stitch, bullion knot) D (overcast stitch)

Spent flowers = A, G, H and I (pistil stitch)

Calyx = D (detached blanket stitch bar)

Beaded blackberries = M, N, O, P and Q (beading)

Sepals = D (needlewoven bar)

Blackberries = A, F, G, H, I, J and K (2 strands, French knot)

Sepals = D (needlewoven bar)

Bows = R

THE FINISHED CUSHION MEASURES 30CM (12") SQUARE.

NEEDLEWOVEN BAR

Needlewoven bars are most often used in needlelace and stumpwork. In flower or fruit embroidery, they make lovely sepals or tiny leaves. Each needlewoven bar is detached from the fabric. It can then be gently manipulated and anchored to the fabric to give the desired effect. We used no. 5 perlé cotton for photographic purposes.

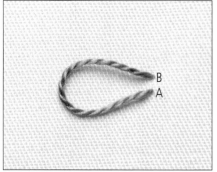

1. Anchor the thread on the back. Bring to the front at A and take to the back at B, leaving a loop of thread the required length on the front.

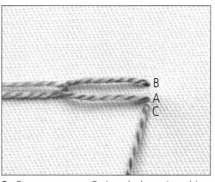

2. Re-emerge at C, just below A, taking care not to pull the loop through. Pass a piece of waste thread through the loop.

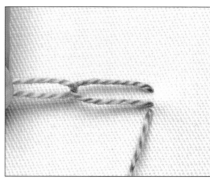

3. With your left hand, hold the waste thread taut, slightly above the surface of the work. Continue to hold this taut while you work.

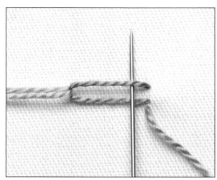

4. Weave the needle over the lower thread of the loop and under the upper thread. Do not pierce the fabric.

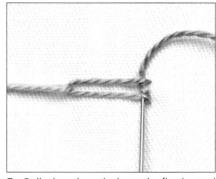

5. Pull the thread through firmly and push the wrap down onto the fabric with the tip of the needle.

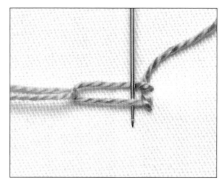

6. Weave the needle over the upper thread and under the lower thread. Do not pierce the fabric.

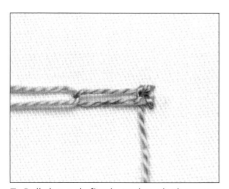

7. Pull through firmly and push the wrap down the loop with the tip of the needle so it sits snugly against the first wrap.

8. Continue working steps 4 to 7, weaving the stitches over and under the threads of the loop. Push each wrap firmly against the previous one.

9. Continue weaving until the loop is completely filled and the wraps are firmly packed.

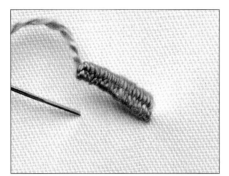

10. Remove the waste thread. Manipulate the sepal and take to the back at the desired position.

11. Pull the thread through. The bar slightly curves and does not lie flat against the fabric.
Completed needlewoven bar.

12. Completed blackberry

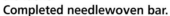

SPENT FLOWER

The spent flowers are worked in pistil stitch with blanket stitch bars as sepals. We used no. 8 perlé cotton for photographic purposes.

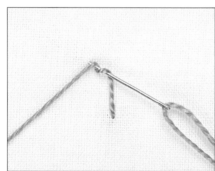

1. Pistil stitch. Bring the thread to the front at A. Holding firmly, wrap the thread over the needle.

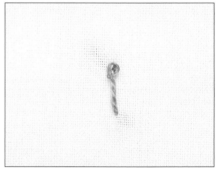

2. Keeping the thread taut, wind it around the needle twice in an anticlockwise direction.

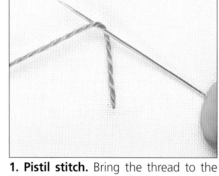

3. Still holding the thread taut, turn it towards the fabric. Place the tip onto the fabric at the marked position for the end of the stitch.

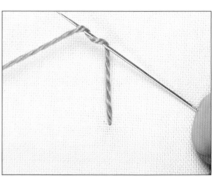

4. Slide the wraps down the needle onto the fabric. Push the needle through the fabric, maintaining a firm tension on the thread.

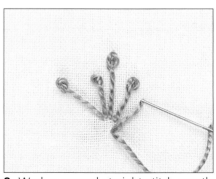

5. Pull the thread through keeping your thumb over the knot.
Completed pistil stitch.

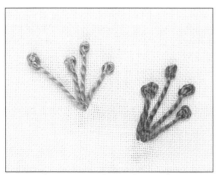

6. Work 7-8 pistil stitches of varying lengths and colour for each flower.

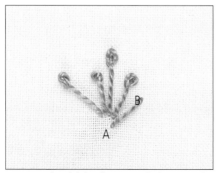

7. Detached blanket stitch bar. Right sepal. Bring the thread to the front at A. Take to the back at B.

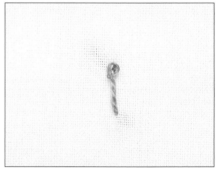

8. Work a second straight stitch exactly over the first.

9. Rotate the work. Bring the needle to the front, just below the straight stitches. Pull the thread through.

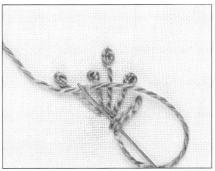

10. Slide the needle under the straight stitches and over the working thread. Do not catch the fabric.

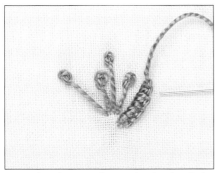

11. Pull the thread towards you until the stitch wraps snugly around the straight stitches.

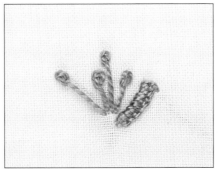

12. Repeat steps 10 and 11 until the straight stitches are completely covered.

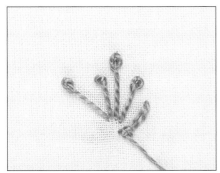

13. Take the needle to the back of the fabric, just below the end of the straight stitches.

14. Pull the thread through. **Completed right sepal.**

15. Left sepal. Bring the needle to the front on the left side of the pistil stitches.

16. Work the left sepal in a similar manner as before. **Completed spent flowers.**

Listen, sweet Dove, unto my song,
And spread thy golden wings in me;
Hatching my tender heart so long,
Till it get wing and fly away with Thee.

~ GEORGE HERBERT,
THE CHURCH ~

GLITTERING DREAMS

by KAREN TORRISI of NEW SOUTH WALES

If beading is your passion, you will love this gorgeous aquamarine cardigan with its
richly decorated neck, front and sleeve bands. Stitched onto a purchased cardigan, the beading is
worked in shades of fuchsia, pink, apricot, gold and silver with beads, sequins and rhinestones
in a delightfully simple floral design.

REQUIREMENTS

Supplies

Aquamarine fine knit cardigan

Aquamarine machine sewing thread

Fine fade-away pen

Tape measure

Beads, Sequins & Needle

See page 62.

THIS DESIGN USES

Beading

PREPARATION FOR EMBROIDERY

We recommend that you read the complete article relating to this project before you begin.

Transferring the design

The centers of the large sequin flowers are marked using the fade-away pen. Mark only four or five flowers at a time to allow for beading before the pen marks fade. Place the tape measure 1.5cm (⅝") from the outer edge and mark at 2.5cm (1") intervals around the neckline and sleeve bands *(diag 1)*. Mark two flowers, evenly spaced, between each buttonhole.

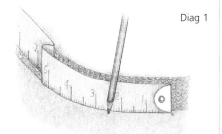

Diag 1

When marking along the neckline, begin at the center back to ensure you have an uneven number of flowers around the neck.

EMBROIDERY

See the liftout pattern for the embroidery diagram.

See page 63 for step-by-step instructions for working the large pink flower and the apricot flower.

Refer to the close-up photograph and embroidery key in the liftout sheet for color placement.

Starting and finishing

Cut 60cm (23 ½") lengths of sewing thread for all beading. Double the thread and thread the tail ends into the needle. Secure the thread with a slip knot at the position of the first bead by taking a small stitch, leaving a loop on the front. Take the needle through the loop *(diag 2)*. Pull taut to anchor the thread.

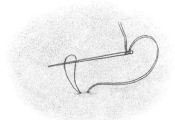

Diag 2

To end off, take the needle to the wrong side and work three small whipping stitches. Trim the thread, leaving a short tail.

Thrice welcome, darling of the Spring! ~ WILLIAM WORDSWORTH

Order of work

Large pink flowers and apricot flowers

The large pink flowers and apricot flowers are worked one at a time. Secure the thread after completing each flower.

From the wrong side of the cardigan, gently ease the claws of a press-in mount (E) through the fabric at each of the marked positions (*diag 3*).

Diag 3

Set a rhinestone (D) into the mount and press the claws firmly down over the stone (*diag 4*).

Diag 4

Embroider the flowers following the step-by-step instructions, alternating between pink and apricot flowers.

Pre-pressed sequin flowers and sequin loops

Referring to the embroidery chart for placement, stitch a flower between each of the large flowers.

Thread a pre-pressed sequin (J) followed by a 5mm (³/₁₆") pink sequin (H) and a silver lined bead (C) onto the needle. Take the needle over the bead and back through the two sequins (*diag 5*).

Diag 5

Work two sequin loops next to each pre-pressed flower in the following manner. Bring the needle to the front close to the flower. Thread C, A, B and J onto the needle. Take the needle to the back approximately 4mm (³/₁₆") from where it emerged (*diag 6*). Work a second sequin loop just next to the first.

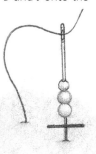

Secure the thread after each group of pre-pressed flower and sequin loops.

Diag 6

Finishing the border

Scatter 4mm (³/₁₆") flat gold sequins (G), stitched in place with C and pink silver lined beads (A), along each side of the flowers. Stitch the leaf shaped rhinestones (F) in place with silver lined beads (C), along each side of the centre front border close to the buttonholes and apricot flowers. Add a rhinestone next to the apricot flower on each side of the front neckline.

Nothing is so beautiful
as Spring -
When weeds, in wheels,
shoot long and lovely and lush...

~ GERARD MANLEY HOPKINS ~

BEADS, RHINESTONES, SEQUINS & NEEDLE

Size 8 seed beads

A = pink silver lined

B = lt gold silver lined

Size 10 seed beads

C = silver lined

Rhinestones

D = 5mm (³/₁₆")
SS20 fuschia (53)

E = 5mm (³/₁₆")
press-in mounts (53)

F = 15mm (⁵/₈") leaf shaped
2669 lt fuschia (15)

4mm (³/₁₆") flat sequins

G = gold (1g)

6mm (¹/₄") flat sequins

H = 1209 pink (10g)

6mm (¹/₄") cup sequins

I = apricot (5g)

8mm (⁵/₁₆") flat sequins

J = light pink AB (5g)

Pre-pressed flower sequins SS22

K = 1cm (³/₈") clear AB (71)

Needle

No. 10 beading

PINK
FLOWER

● ● ●

Each petal is stitched with
a triple sequin loop sitting
flat against the fabric.

1. Secure the thread with a
slip knot half the width of a
bead (C) above the centre
rhinestone.

2. Slide C, C, H, C, H, C and
H onto the thread.

3. Take the needle to the back
three quarters the width of a
sequin away from where it
emerged.

4. Pull the thread through.
The outermost sequin should
lie flat against the fabric and
the innermost should stand up.

5. Repeat at the remaining
three compass points around
the centre, bringing the
thread to the front half a
bead's width from the
rhinestone.

6. Bring the thread to the
front between two compass
points. Work a petal in the
same manner as before.

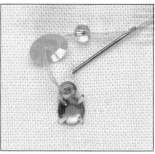

7. Pull the thread through.
Repeat for the remaining
petals.

APRICOT
FLOWER

● ● ●

Each petal is stitched
with a single raised cup
sequin.

1. Secure the thread with a
slip knot half a bead's width
above the center rhinestone.

2. Thread on A, I and B,
ensuring the right side of the
sequin is facing up when you
pick it up with the needle.

3. Take the needle to the back
half the width of the sequin
away from where it emerged.

4. Pull the thread through.
The sequin will stand up at an
angle over the outer bead.

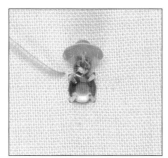

5. Bring the thread to the
front next to the pink bead,
half a bead's width from the
rhinestone.

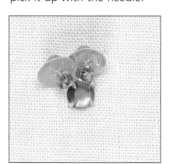

6. Work a second petal in the
same manner.

7. Work another five petals
around the center rhinestone
in this manner. The sequins
will overlap slightly.

CAPRICE

by SUSAN O'CONNOR of VICTORIA

Black silk forms a dramatic background for the exotic floral design on this stylish
evening bag. Lustrous silk flowers and leaves, surrounded by beaded berries
and flashing sequins, create a rich, opulent surface.
The bag is lined with aubergine satin and sits on small pink feet.

REQUIREMENTS

Fabric

40cm (15 ¾") square
of black silk dupioni

40cm (15 ¾") square of
aubergine satin

Supplies

80cm x 40cm wide (31 ½" x 15 ¾")
piece of black woven fusible interfacing

14cm (5 ½") gold metal purse frame

14cm x 5cm wide (5 ½" x 2") piece
of template plastic

25cm (10") embroidery hoop

Tissue paper

Sharp lead pencil

Threads, Beads, Sequins and Needles

See page 69.

THIS DESIGN USES

Beading · Chain stitch
Detached chain · French knot
Ghiordes knot
Long and short stitch
Padded satin stitch
Satin stitch · Split stitch
Straight stitch · Stem stitch
Wrapping

PREPARATION FOR EMBROIDERY

See the liftout pattern for the
embroidery design and pattern. See
page 119 for the cutting layout.

Cut out the black silk piece for the
handle following the cutting layout. The
remaining piece of silk is cut to its exact
shape after the embroidery is complete.

Transferring the design

Using the lead pencil, trace the design,
cutting lines, stitch lines and placement
marks onto tissue paper.

Fuse the piece of interfacing for the bag
onto the wrong side of the black silk.
Position the tracing over the silk, aligning
the placement marks with the straight
grain of the fabric. Pin in place.

Using contrasting sewing thread, tack
along the design, cutting and stitch lines
using small stitches. Moisten the paper,
wait a few seconds then tear away.

Place the fabric in the hoop.

THE FINISHED BAG (EXCLUDING THE HANDLE) MEASURES 13.5CM X 21CM WIDE (5 ¼" X 8 ¼").

EMBROIDERY

Refer to the embroidery key and close-up photograph for color placement. See pages 70 to 73 for the step-by-step instructions for the yellow berries, small blue flower spray, large pink flower and attaching the frame to the bag.

All embroidery is worked before the bag is constructed.

Use the sharp needle for the beading and the milliner's needle for the blackberries. Use the crewel needle for wrapping the yellow berries and for all other embroidery.

Order of work

Stems

Using the mahogany silk thread and beginning at the base of the stems, work a row of stem stitch to the base of the second leaf on the left hand side and to the first leaf on the right hand side. Work a row using tobacco silk on each side of the first row. Complete the main stems, tapering to a single row at the ends *(diag 1)*.

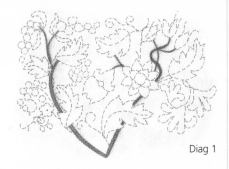

Diag 1

Work the purple berry stems, beginning with three rows and tapering to a single row. Embroider the yellow berry stems using tobacco silk. Work a brown bud using two strands of tobacco at the tip of each stem. Finish each bud with a French knot at the base.

Leaves

Outline each leaf with the dark yellow green silk.

Beginning with the avocado green along the centre vein, embroider the leaves in long and short stitch, blending each color into the previous one. Using two strands of mahogany, work the leaf stems.

Large pink flower

Work the large pink flower following the step-by-step instructions.

Large pink bud

Outline the petals and calyx in split stitch. Embroider the petals and calyx in long and short stitch, covering the split stitch outline. Refer to the close-up photograph for color placement.

Work the receptacle and the remaining area below the petals in padded satin stitch using the darkest green. Outline the outer petals and calyx in stem stitch. Using two strands of thread, work the stem. Attach three beads at the tip of the bud.

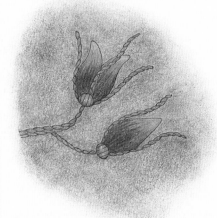

Small buds

Outline each bud with colonial gold. Beginning with purple grape silk at the base, fill each bud with long and short stitch finishing with colonial gold at the tip. Using the darkest green, work each receptacle in padded satin stitch. Embroider the sepals in stem stitch *(diag 2)*.

Diag 2

For the largest of the buds, finish four of the sepals with a detached chain.

Stitch the stems using two strands of dark avocado green.

Large blue flowers

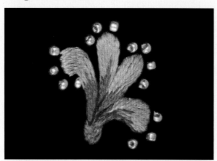

Outline the two blue flowers with lavender blue silk and the green flower with yellow-green. Using the photograph as a guide for color placement, fill each petal with long and short stitch. Embroider the receptacle at the base of the blue flowers. Stitch the stems with two strands of tobacco silk. Attach gold beads around the petals.

Blackberries

The berries are stitched in various combinations of colors *(diag 3)*.

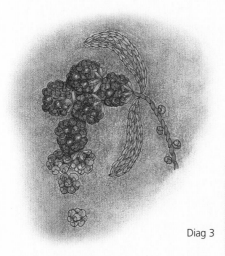

Diag 3

With five strands of the darkest mauve, work French knots over most of the larger berries and along one side of the medium berries. Use two strands of the darkest mauve blended together with three strands of the lighter shade to fill the remainder of the large and part of the medium berries with French knots. Using five strands of the lighter shade, fill the remaining areas of the medium berries.

Embroider the small berries in the same manner, using five strands of the lighter shade of mauve for the top half. Use three strands of the lighter mauve blended with two strands of bright yellow-green for the lower half. Stitch the smallest berries on the left spray with five strands of bright yellow-green. Scatter dark red French knots over the large and medium berries. Stitch one to three blue seed beads onto the larger berries. Embroider three to five celery green straight stitches at the top of some berries for sepals.

Outline each leaf in chain stitch and work a row of stem stitch along the center. Stitch French knots along each stem.

Yellow berries

Make ten beaded berries following the step-by-step instructions.

Work the remaining berries in padded satin stitch, attaching a bead to each of the three larger berries. Using two strands of dark green, work French knots at the top of each berry. Work one or two French knots along the end of each stem.

Small blue flower spray

Embroider the dark green stem.

Work the flowers, buds and leaves following the step-by-step instructions.

Tendrils

Embroider the two dark green tendrils in stem stitch, keeping the stitches short as you work around the tight curves.

Sequins

Scatter silver sequins among the flowers and on the back of the bag. Using a single strand of cranberry, attach each sequin to the fabric with a red seed bead. Secure the thread on the back before moving to the next position.

CONSTRUCTION

See pages 119 and 120.

THREADS, BEADS, SEQUINS & NEEDLES

Au Ver à Soie, Soie d'Alger
A = 243 bright yellow-green
B = 516 vy dk avocado green
C = 636 vy dk rust
D = 1831 vy lt celery green
E = 2145 dk yellow-green
F = 2243 colonial gold
G = 2514 autumn yellow
H = 2926 vy dk brick red
I = 3336 vy dk purple grape
J = 4635 dk gray-mauve

K = 4636 vy dk gray-mauve
L = 4912 lt lavender blue
Madeira stranded silk
M = 0703 cranberry
N = 0812 shell pink
O = 0813 lt shell pink
P = 2008 mahogany
Q = 2113 tobacco
Mill Hill glass seed beads
R = 00168 sapphire
S = 00557 gold

T = 02011 Victorian gold
U = 03048 cinnamon red
Mill Hill pebble beads
V = 05021 silver (14 beads)
Sequins 5mm (³/₁₆")
W = vintage silver sequins
(27 sequins)
Needles
No. 3 milliner's
No. 9 crewel
No. 12 sharp

EMBROIDERY KEY

All embroidery is worked with one strand unless otherwise specified.
Stems = P or Q (2 strands, stem stitch, satin stitch, French knot)
Leaves = E (split stitch), B, E and F (long and short stitch)
P (2 strands, stem stitch)

Large pink flower
Outer petals = M (split stitch)
H, M and O
(long and short stitch)
Outline = C (stem stitch)
Inner petals = M (split stitch)
M and O (long and short stitch)
Outline = H (stem stitch)
Center = G (2 strands
Ghiordes knot), G and T (beading)

Large pink bud
Outer petals = M (split stitch)
F, H and M (long and short stitch)
Outline = C (stem stitch)
Center petal = M (split stitch)
M and O (split stitch
long and short stitch)
Calyx = H (split stitch)
C, F, H and I (long and short stitch)

Base of petals = B
(padded satin stitch)
Outline = B (stem stitch)
Receptacle = B
(padded satin stitch)
Stem = B (2 strands, stem stitch)
Beads = G and T (beading)

Small buds
Bud = F (split stitch), C, F, H and I
(long and short stitch)
Receptacle = B
(padded satin stitch)
Sepals = B
(stem stitch, detached chain)
Stem = B (2 strands, stem stitch)

Large blue flowers
Petals = E or L (split stitch)
B, E, I, J, K, L and O
(long and short stitch)
Receptacle = B (satin stitch)
Stem = Q (2 strands, stem stitch)
Beads = G and S (beading)

Blackberries
Berry = A, J and K (2 - 5 strands
French knot), H (2 strands
French knot), R (beading)

Sepals = D
(2 strands, straight stitch)
Leaves = D (2 strands, chain stitch)
B (2 strands, stem stitch)
Stem spots = D
(2 strands, French knot)

Yellow berries
Berry = G, U and V
(wrapped bead, beading), G and U
(padded satin stitch, beading)
Calyx = B
(2 strands, French knot)

Small blue flower spray
Stem = B (2 strands, stem stitch)
Petals = L
(split stitch, padded satin stitch)
Petal markings = N and O
(straight stitch), S (beading)
Pink bud = O
(2 strands, French knot)
Sepals = B
(2 strands, detached chain or
straight stitch, French knot)
Leaves = B
(2 strands, detached chain)
Tendrils = B
(2 strands, stem stitch)
Sequins = M, W and U (beading)

YELLOW BERRIES

We used a contrasting pebble bead for photographic purposes.

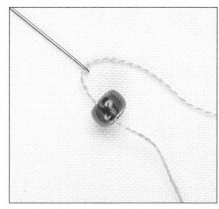

1. Cut a 100cm (40") length of G. Using the crewel needle and leaving a 15cm (6") tail, take the thread through the bead.

2. Holding the thread tail securely, take the needle and thread up through the bead, wrapping the bead firmly.

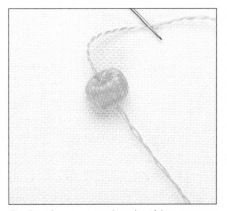

3. Continue wrapping in this manner, until the bead is densely covered.

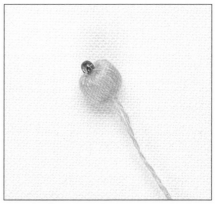

4. Thread a red seed bead onto the needle. Take the thread back through the covered bead and secure at the base.

5. Attaching the berry. Thread both tails into the needle and stitch securely in place.

SMALL BLUE FLOWER SPRAY

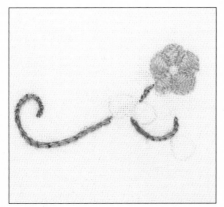

1. Outline the flower petals in split stitch. Work the layers of satin stitch padding.

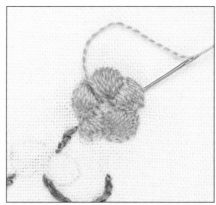

2. Cover the flower petals with satin stitch, working from the centre, over the outline.

3. Work several straight stitches radiating from the base of each petal with N. Place a straight stitch in O between each petal.

4. Embroider the buds in padded satin stitch in a similar manner to the petals.

5. Using N and O, work several straight stitches at the base of the large bud petals. Using O, repeat for the small bud.

6. Work a French knot at the tip of the stem. Attach a bead at the center of the open flower.

7. Stitch the sepals on the larger bud with detached chain, worked with a long anchoring stitch and a French knot at the base of the bud.

8. Stitch the sepals on the small bud with straight stitches. Stitch the smallest leaf with a detached chain.

9. Work the medium leaf with two detached chains, one inside the other, and the largest leaf with three detached chains.

LARGE PINK FLOWER

1. Outline all the petals of the flower in split stitch.

2. Beginning at the tip of each petal, cover with long and short stitch, covering the split stitch outline.

3. Outline the petals with stem stitch, using C for the outer petals and H for the inner petals.

4. Fill the center of the flower with close rows of Ghiordes knots, stitched with two strands of G.

5. Cut and comb the knots to form a dense mound.

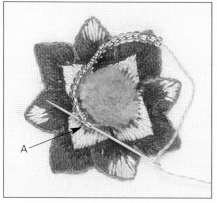

6. Bring the needle to the front at A. Thread enough beads onto the needle to form a circle. Take the needle back through the first bead in the same direction.

7. Take the needle to the back. Re-emerge between two beads and couch the circle in place.

ATTACHING THE FRAME TO THE BAG

Follow the instructions in the liftout sheet to construct the bag and lining. We used contrasting fabrics and thread for photographic purposes.

1. Fold 1cm (3/8") to the wrong side at the top of the bag and the lining and press.

2. Place the lining inside the bag. Pin and tack together.

3. Overcast the two layers together along the top edge. Remove the pins and tacking.

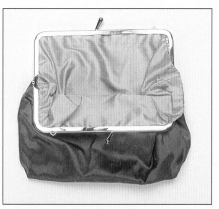

4. Open the frame. Push the edges of the bag into the frame.

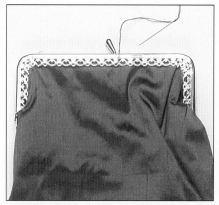

5. Using strong black thread and beginning at the center, bring the needle to the front through the filigree on the frame.

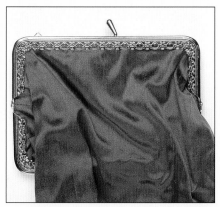

6. Stitch the frame to the top of the bag through the filigree edge using back stitch. Stop 1cm (³⁄₈") from the side seam.

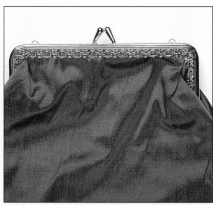

7. Return to the center. Stitch the other half in the same manner. Attach the second side of the frame in the same manner.

Back of bag

REJOICE

by CAROLYN PEARCE of NEW SOUTH WALES

Gleaming metallic threads, glistening beads and brass charms all combine to create this lavish Christmas bell. Worked onto Thai silk in a myriad of stitches, both simple and complex, this elegant bell will make a perfect decoration for the festive season. The bell is finished with an ornate beaded tassel and hangs from a twisted gold cord.

REQUIREMENTS

Fabric

30cm (12") square of ivory Thai silk

30cm (12") square of quilter's muslin

Supplies

3 x 1cm (³⁄₈") brass snowflake charms

Fiber-fill

White beading thread

Clear nylon thread

Cream quilting thread

25cm (10") embroidery hoop
inner ring bound

11cm x 4cm wide (4 ³⁄₈" x 1 ½") piece
of thin card

Tracing paper

Sharp HB pencil

Threads, Beads & Needles

See page 78.

THIS DESIGN USES

Armenian edging stitch · Back stitch
Basque stitch · Beading · Breton stitch
Cross stitch flower · Detached chain
Knotted cable chain
Knotted pearl stitch · Outline stitch
Portuguese knotted stem stitch
Raised cross stitch flower
Straight stitch
Whipped reverse chain stitch

PREPARATION FOR EMBROIDERY

See the liftout pattern for the embroidery designs.

Neaten the raw edges of the silk and quilter's muslin with a machine zigzag or overlock stitch to prevent fraying.

Fold the piece of silk in half. Using a light coloured sewing thread, tack along the foldline. Unfold the silk. Do not cut the silk until the embroidery is complete.

Transferring the designs

Using a fine black pen, trace the front and back designs, stitch lines, cutting lines and placement marks onto the one piece of tracing paper. Place the tracing over a window or light box and tape in place. Center the silk over the tracing, aligning the placement marks with the row of tacking. Pin in place. The light shining through will make the designs

---

Let's dance and sing and make good cheer, For Christmas comes but once a year.

~ SIR GEORGE ALEXANDER MACFARREN, FROM A FRAGMENT (BEFORE 1580) ~

'Ring out the old, ring in the new, Ring, happy bells, across the snow.'

~ ALFRED LORD TENNYSON, IN MEMORIAM ~

---

visible through the fabric. Using the pencil, lightly trace the designs, stitch lines and cutting lines onto the fabric *(diag 1)*.

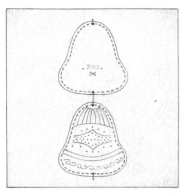

Diag 1

Place the silk over the muslin, aligning the straight grain of the fabrics. Tack the fabrics together, 5cm (2") from all edges. Place the fabrics in the hoop.

EMBROIDERY

See pages 79 - 83 for the step-by-step instructions for Armenian edging stitch, Basque stitch, Breton stitch, cross stitch flower, knotted cable chain, raised cross stitch flower and whipped reverse chain stitch.

Refer to the embroidery key and close-up photograph for color placement.

See the embroidery chart in the liftout sheet for stitch placement.

Use the beading thread for all beading, the nylon thread for attaching the brass snowflake charms and the quilting thread for tying and beading the tassel. Use the crewel needle for the beading, the no. 6 between for the fine metallic threads and the no. 4 between for the remaining threads. Use the tapestry needle for constructing the tassel.

Order of work

Front

Upper section

Following the step-by-step instructions, embroider a row of Basque stitch along the upper and lower edge of the top section. Keep the chains approx 2.5mm (1/12") long and facing outwards. Fill in the shape with vertical rows of knotted pearl stitch, keeping the stitches 2mm (1/16") wide. Work Breton stitch in the spaces between the rows following the step-by-step instructions.

Middle section

Upper row

Following the step-by-step instructions, embroider a cross stitch flower at each of the marked positions.

Attach a group of four beads in the spaces between the flowers and at each end of the row. To attach each bead, keep the stitch as long as the length of the bead *(diag 2)*.

Diag 2

Re-emerge through the first hole and pass the needle through the thread loop *(diag 3)*.

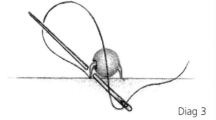

Diag 3

Pull firmly and take the needle to the back through the same hole in the fabric. This will keep the bead upright and in the exact position.

Center row

Following the step-by-step instructions, embroider a row of knotted cable chain above and below the center row.

The triangular shapes on each side of the center beads are worked as groups of four straight stitches.

Work the first stitch from the upper left dot to just above the center dot to allow room for the bead *(diag 4)*.

Diag 4

Stitch another two stitches in the space before the next dot. Work the fourth stitch from the second dot to the center. Re-emerge through the second dot to work the first stitch in the next group of four stitches *(diag 5)*.

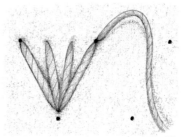

Diag 5

Continue in this manner across the band and repeat for the lower row of triangles. Attach a bead in each space between the tips of the groups of stitches *(diag 6)*.

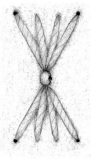

Diag 6

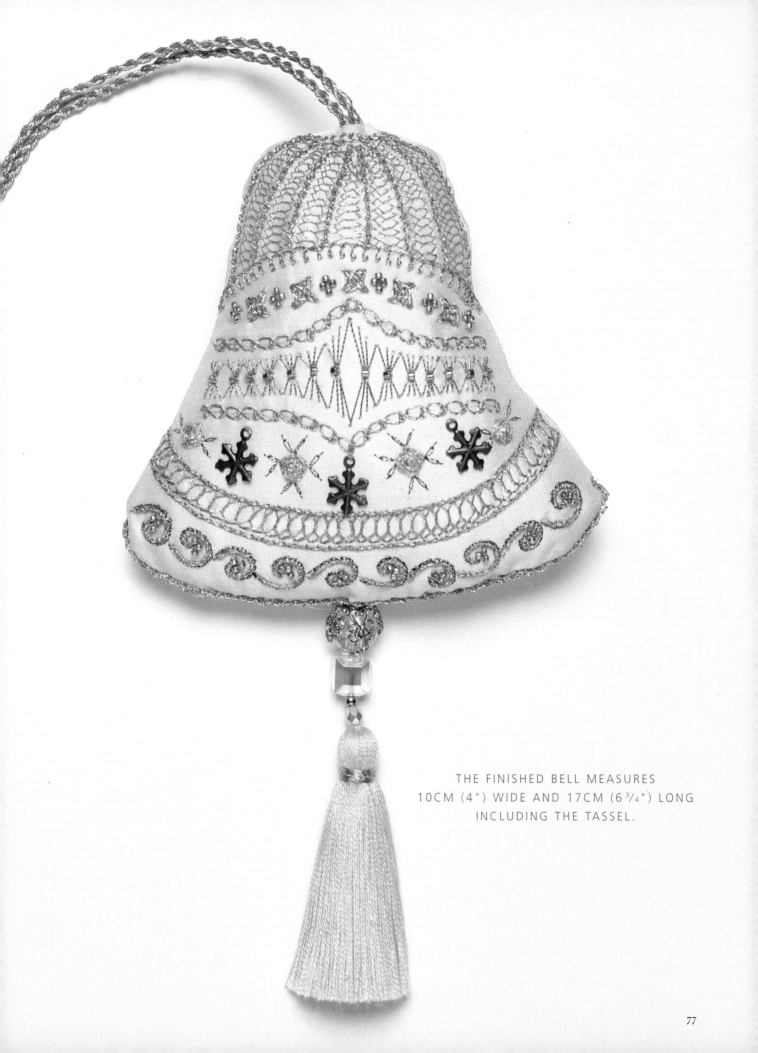

THE FINISHED BELL MEASURES
10CM (4") WIDE AND 17CM (6¾") LONG
INCLUDING THE TASSEL.

Lower row

Following the step-by-step instructions, embroider four raised cross stitch flowers at the marked positions, making the upright cross 4mm (³⁄₁₆") wide. Use the eye end of the needle to manipulate the stitches around the spokes. Stitch four pairs of detached chain leaves, each with a long anchoring stitch, around each flower. The bronze snowflake charms are attached between the flowers after the embroidery is complete.

Lower section

Upper band

Work a row of Breton stitch along the upper band, taking the needle through the fabric just inside the marked lines.

Following the step-by-step instructions, stitch a row of whipped reverse chain stitch along the marked lines.

Scrolls

Working from the left hand side, embroider the scrolls in Portuguese knotted stem stitch. Ensure you have sufficient thread in the needle to complete each scroll. Work a row of outline stitch along the outside of each scroll and attach three petite beads at the tips.

The edging is worked in Armenian edging stitch over the lower seam line, after the bell is constructed.

Back

Date

Embroider the year of completion in tiny back stitches. Work two raised cross stitch flowers, each surrounded by a pair of detached chain leaves, at each side. Stitch two pairs of detached chain leaves below the date.

CONSTRUCTION

See pages 120 and 121.

Hints

It is preferable to use a round eyed needle for metallic threads, as it is less likely to cut the thread at the eye.

When learning a new stitch, it is advisable to practise on a scrap of fabric. Evenweave fabrics make it easier to achieve even stitches while practising.

THREADS, BEADS & NEEDLES

Threads

Au Ver à Soie Metallics Antique

A = 901 black-gold

Au Ver à Soie Metallics Bourdon

B = 1102 gold

C = 3002 antique gold

Kreinik Metallic very fine (#4) braid

D = 102 Vatican

Papillon thread

E = gold

YLI silk floss

F = 182 ivory (2 skeins)

Beads

Mill Hill petite glass beads

G = 40557 gold

Maria George Delica beads

H = DBR 31 metallic bright gold

Beads for tassel

2mm (¹⁄₁₆") gold spacers (2 beads)

3mm (¹⁄₈") metallic cream crystal

7mm (⁵⁄₁₆") square Swarovski crystal AB

10mm (³⁄₈") clear crystal

10mm (³⁄₈") gold filigree bead cap

Needles

No. 4 between

No. 6 between

No. 10 crewel

No. 26 tapestry

EMBROIDERY KEY

All embroidery is worked with one strand unless otherwise specified.

Front

Upper section

Outlines = C (Basque stitch)

Filling = E (3 strands, knotted pearl stitch), B (Breton stitch)

Middle section

Upper row = E (3 strands, cross stitch flowers), G (beading)

Center row = E (3 strands, knotted cable chain), C (straight stitch)
H (beading)

Lower row = D (raised cross stitch flower), A (detached chain)

Lower section

Upper row = E (3 strands, Breton stitch)
B (whipped reverse chain)

Scrolls = E (2 strands, Portuguese knotted stem stitch)
A (outline stitch), G (beading)

Edging = E (3 strands, Armenian edging stitch)

Back

Date = E (back stitch)

Flowers = D (raised cross stitch flowers)
A (detached chain)

ARMENIAN EDGING STITCH

• • •

Embroidered in metallic thread and with a second row of detached stitches, this stitch creates a narrow scalloped edge. Work with a 30cm (12") length of thread to avoid starting a new thread half way along the row. The stitch is worked from left to right. We used no. 5 perlé cotton for photographic purposes.

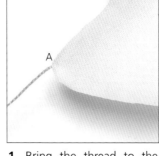

1. Bring the thread to the front of the seam line at A.

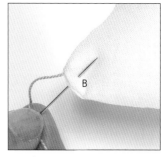

2. Take a small stitch through the seam, re-emerging at B.

3. Twist the thread loop to the right, forming a figure eight. Take the needle under and through the lower loop.

4. Pull the stitch firmly to form a knot. Completed first stitch.

5. Repeat steps 2 - 4, at 3mm (⅛") intervals, to the end of the row. Take the needle through the seam at C, a short distance from the last knot, and secure.

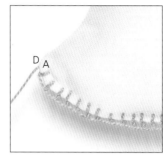

6. Detached Armenian edging stitch. Bring the thread to the front at D, just to the left of A.

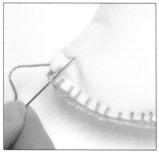

7. Pass the needle under the loop of the first stitch in the first row.

8. Repeat step 3.

9. Pull the thread firmly, forming a knot around the loop of the first stitch.

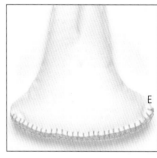

10. Continue to work the knots into the loops of the first row. End off at E a short distance from the last knot.

BASQUE STITCH

This delicate edging stitch looks like a row of tiny drops. We used no. 5 perlé cotton for photographic purposes.

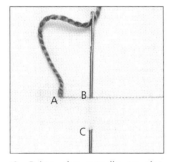

1. Bring the needle to the front at A. Pull the thread through and take a stitch from B to C, keeping the thread above the needle.

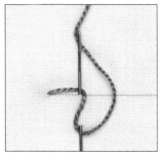

2. Take the thread from left to right behind the eye end and under the tip of the needle. Pull the thread firmly.

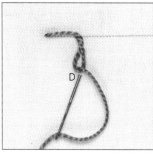

3. Pull the thread through. Take the needle to the back at D, anchoring the thread loop.

4. Bring the needle to the front at B, through the same hole in the fabric.

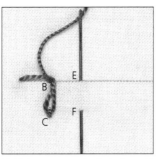

5. Take a second stitch from E to F, ensuring the distance is the same as B to C.

6. Complete the second stitch following steps 2 and 3, anchoring the chain at G and re-emerging at E.

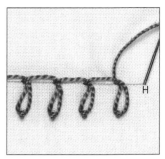

7. Continue in this manner to the end of the row. To end off, take the thread to the back at H a short distance from the last chain.

BRETON STITCH

This is a wide border stitch, worked between two lines. The stitches overlap along the lower edge and sit side-by-side along the upper edge. We used no. 5 perlé cotton for photographic purposes.

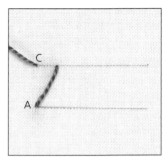

1. Bring the thread to the front at A on the lower line. Take the needle to the back at B, on the upper line.

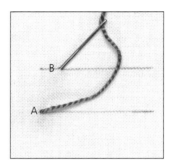

2. Pull the thread through keeping the stitch relaxed. Re-emerge at C, directly above A.

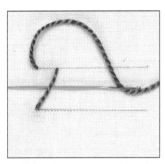

3. Take the needle under the stitch from right to left. Do not pierce the fabric.

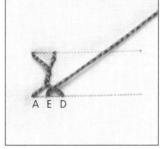

4. Take the needle to the back at D on the lower line and to the right of B. Pull the thread through. **Completed first stitch.**

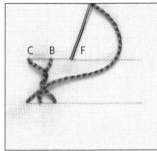

5. Re-emerge at E on the lower line, halfway between A and D.

6. Take the needle to the back at F. The distance between B and F must be the same as B and C.

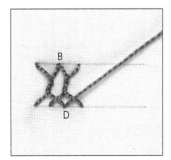

7. Re-emerge at B, through the same hole in the fabric. Complete the second stitch following steps 3 and 4. Re-emerge at D.

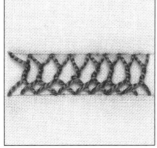

8. Continue in this manner to the end of the row, ensuring the spacing of the stitches is kept even.

9. To work along a curved line, work the stitches slightly wider along the outer edge of the curve.

CROSS STITCH FLOWER

These flowers are worked as two cross stitches with the top stitch interwoven with the first. The flowers on the bell are worked with four cross stitches creating a larger flower. We used no. 5 perlé cotton for photographic purposes.

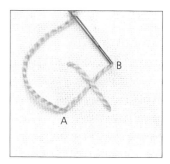

1. Work a cross stitch between the points of the flower.

2. Take a stitch from A to B, over the first stitch and through the same holes in the fabric.

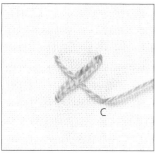

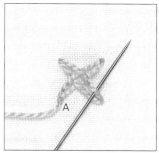

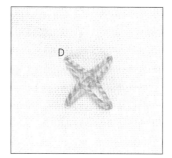

3. Pull the thread through, keeping the stitch to the right of the first stitch. Re-emerge at C.

4. Weave the needle over the previous stitch and under the first stitch.

5. Take the needle to the back at D. Pull the thread through, keeping the stitches side-by-side. **Completed cross stitch flower.**

6. Double cross stitch flower. Bring the thread to the front at A. Keeping the needle to the right, weave over and under the previous stitches.

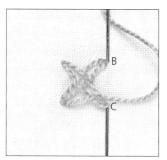

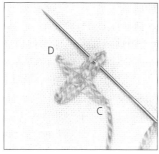

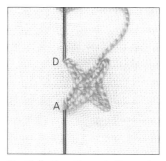

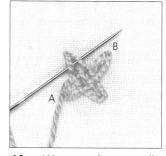

7. Pull the thread through. Take a stitch from B to C.

8. Weave the needle from C to D above the previous stitch (under, over, under).

9. Pull the thread through. Take a stitch from D to A.

10. Weave the needle from A to B above the previous stitches (under, over, under).

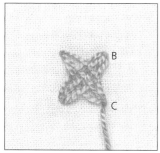

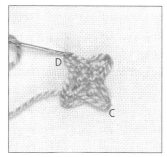

I heard the bells on Christmas Day

Their old, familiar carols play,

And wild and sweet

The words repeat

Of peace on earth, goodwill to men!

~ HENRY WADSWORTH LONGFELLOW, CHRISTMAS BELLS ~

11. Pull the thread through. Take the needle to the back at B. Re-emerge at C.

12. Weave the needle from C to D below the previous stitches (over, under, over, under). Take the needle to the back at D. **Completed double cross stitch flower.**

KNOTTED CABLE CHAIN

This effective line stitch is a combination of coral stitch and chain stitch. It produces a row of chains interlocked by knots. The stitch is worked from right to left.
We used no. 5 perlé cotton for photographic purposes.

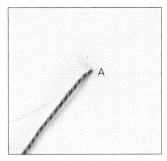

1. Bring the thread to the front at A on the line to be covered. Hold the thread in place along the line.

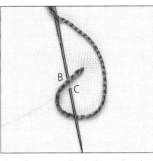

2. Take a small stitch under the line and the laid thread from B to C. The loop of the thread is under the tip of the needle.

3. Pull the thread through, making a coral knot. Take the needle under the first stitch without picking up any fabric.

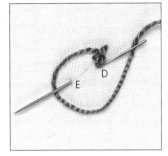

4. Loop the thread to the left. Take a stitch from D (next to the knot) to E on the line. Keep the thread under the needle tip.

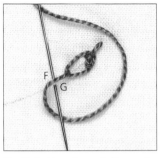

5. Pull the thread through, making a chain. Take the needle from F to G, under the laid thread and over the loop.

6. Pull the thread through. Take the needle under the stitch between the chain and the second knot.

7. Pull the thread through. Stitch a chain, taking the needle from H to I, keeping the thread under the tip of the needle.

8. Continue following steps 5 - 7. To end off, work a knot after the last chain and take the needle to the back between the last knot and chain.

RAISED CROSS STITCH FLOWER

This flower is worked over the four spokes created by an upright cross. The arrow indicates the top of the fabric. We used no. 5 perlé cotton for photographic purposes.

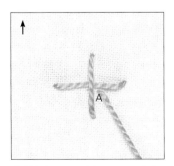

1. Work an upright cross stitch. Bring the needle to the front at A at the center, just below and to the right of the cross.

2. Take the needle under the right spoke, without picking up any fabric. Keep the thread under the needle tip.

 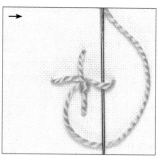  

3. Pull the thread through around the spoke of the cross.

4. Turn the fabric 90 degrees to the right. Take the needle under the next spoke in the same manner.

5. Work over the remaining spokes, turning the fabric for each stitch. Ensure the stitches lie closely around the center. **Completed first round.**

6. Continue in this manner around the spokes until the cross is covered. Take the needle under the flower and secure. **Completed raised cross stitch flower.**

WHIPPED REVERSE CHAIN STITCH

● ● ●

Rows of whipped reverse chain stitch border the Breton stitch on the lower section of the bell.

It is essential to work with a firm thread to achieve the correct effect. A line of reverse chain stitch forms the foundation row. We used no.5 perlé cotton in contrasting colours for photographic purposes.

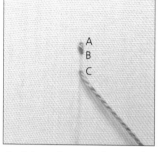 

1. Bring the needle to the front at A. Take it to the back at B and re-emerge at C, 2mm (¹⁄₁₆") from B.

2. Pass the needle under the first stitch and take it to the back at C. Pull the thread through.

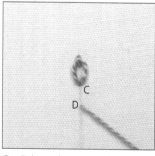 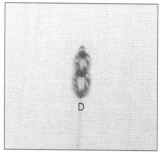 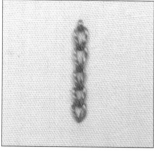 

3. Bring the needle to the front at D, 2mm (¹⁄₁₆") from C.

4. Pass the needle and thread under the first chain without catching the fabric. Take the thread to the back at D.

5. Continue stitching in this manner to the end of the row.

6. Whipping. Using a second thread, bring the needle to the front inside the first chain on the design line.

7. Slide the needle under the left half of this chain. Do not go through the fabric.

8. Pull the thread through. Slide the needle from right to left under the second chain.

9. Pull the thread through until the whipped stitch rests gently against the chain stitch.

10. Continue in the same manner. To end off, take the thread to the back under the last chain. **Completed whipped reverse chain.**

TAKING TEA

by HELAN PEARCE of VICTORIA

This gorgeous beaded teapot brings to mind memories of spring gardens in full bloom and tea parties on the lawn. Jacobean inspired surface embroidery has been cleverly combined with beading and stumpwork to create this amazing picture.

REQUIREMENTS

Fabric

40cm (15 ¾") square of off-white silk dupioni

40cm (15 ¾") square of white cotton lawn

Supplies

40cm (15 ¾") square of shapewell

15cm x 75cm (6" x 29 ½") piece of medium weight non-woven interfacing eg Vilene

40cm (15 ¾") square of medium weight wadding eg Pellon

White beading thread

Small amount of fiber-fill

110cm (43 ¼") 32 gauge beading wire

130cm (51 ¼") 30 gauge green covered wire

Fine black pen

Sharp HB pencil

Fine water-soluble fabric marker

Wire cutters or old scissors

10cm (4") embroidery hoop

25cm (10") embroidery hoop

Threads, Beads & Needles

See page 89.

THIS DESIGN USES

Beading · Blanket stitch · Chain stitch
Closed herringbone stitch
Cross stitch · Detached chain
Feather stitch · Fly stitch
French knot · Granitos
Long and short blanket stitch
Long and short stitch
Palestrina stitch · Pistil stitch · Quilting
Satin stitch · Seed stitch · Stem stitch
Straight stitch · Trellis couching
Whipping · Whipped stem stitch

PREPARATION FOR EMBROIDERY

See the liftout pattern for the embroidery design and templates for the detached leaves and petals.

Neaten the raw edges of the silk with a machine zigzag or overlock stitch to prevent fraying.

Transferring the design

Using the black pen, trace the design and placement marks onto the tracing paper. With the right side facing up, center the silk fabric over the tracing, aligning the placement marks with the straight grain of the fabric. Tape in place. Using the pencil, carefully trace the design onto the fabric.

Tack the piece of shapewell to the wrong side of the silk, aligning the straight grain of the fabrics. Place the prepared fabrics in the large hoop.

THE FINISHED DESIGN MEASURES 19CM X 17CM WIDE (7 ½" X 6 ¾").

EMBROIDERY

See pages 90 and 91 for the step-by-step instructions for palestrina stitch and detached petals.

Refer to the embroidery key and close-up photograph for color placement.

The wired leaves, tendrils and petals are worked separately before being attached to the fabric.

Use the beading needle for all beading and the sharp needle when stitching the gold highlights and quilting the design outline. Use the no. 7 crewel needle for the 2 ply silk thread and the no. 8 crewel needle for all other embroidery.

All embroidery is worked with the fabric in a hoop.

Order of work

Center motif

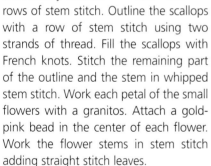

Work the band across the motif with closely worked rows of stem stitch. Outline the scallops with a row of stem stitch using two strands of thread. Fill the scallops with French knots. Stitch the remaining part of the outline and the stem in whipped stem stitch. Work each petal of the small flowers with a granitos. Attach a gold-pink bead in the center of each flower. Work the flower stems in stem stitch adding straight stitch leaves.

Left hand motif

Outline the lower half of the motif in palestrina stitch following the step-by-step instructions. Work the upper half of the outline in whipped stem stitch. Cover the scroll with close rows of French knots. Beginning at the tip, work the center vein in feather stitch and work a French knot at the tip of each stitch. Work evenly spaced detached chains over the lower half of the motif.

Right hand motif

For the trellis, work three long, evenly spaced straight stitches across the round part of the motif. Stitch a second layer of three stitches over the first in the opposite direction. Couch each intersection in place with a tiny stitch. Beginning at the base, embroider a row of stem stitch for the center vein. Work evenly spaced pistil stitches on the left side of the vein. Starting at the top of the motif, work the left outline in feather stitch. Outline the couched trellis with a row of whipped stem stitch. Attach a bead in each diamond of the trellis. Work two satin stitch leaves at the base of the motif.

Upper motif

Work the trellis inside the paisley in a similar manner to the right hand motif.

Embroider the outline of the paisley section in whipped stem stitch. Outline the motif in palestrina stitch, using toucan along the upper section and pansy around the two petals on the right side.

Embroider a granitos for each of the leaves along the small branches. Stitch a detached chain around each granitos and work the stems in stem stitch. Work three granitos buds along the upper edge of the motif and two multi color lavender granitos to the right of the paisley.

Embroider the three green leaves in fly stitch with stem stitch stems.

Beginning along the outline and working towards the center, cover the lower half of the leaf on the right of the paisley with closely worked rows of stem stitch. Stitch

closed herringbone stitch across the upper half of the leaf and work the outline in whipped stem stitch. Embroider the stem in feather stitch, working from the base of the leaf to the paisley.

Lower left motif

Cover the motif with a trellis in the same manner as before. Couch each intersection with a tiny gold cross stitch. Outline the shape and work the stem in whipped stem stitch. Beginning at the tip, embroider the tendril in feather stitch.

Lower center motif

Starting at the tip of the scroll, outline the upper section of the motif in stem stitch. Cover the shape with satin stitch, working over the stem stitch outline. Using gold, whip the stem stitch scroll and add straight stitches over the satin stitch. Stitch a row of whipped stem stitch along the lower edge of the middle section. Fill the section with seed stitch. Work whipped stem stitch along the lower edge of the remaining section of the motif. Embroider three clusters, each with five pistil stitches, in a fan shape. Work a fly stitch around the base of each cluster *(diag 1)*.

Embroider the green leaf in the same manner as before.

Diag 1

Lower right motif

Using gilded lavender, embroider three sprays of granitos leaves in the paisley section in the same manner as the upper motif. Work the remaining set of tiny leaves in variegated mauve.

Working from the tip of the right section, work a row of stem stitch to the base of the mauve leaf spray. Continue to work close rows of stem stitch to cover the lower part of the motif. Add straight gold stitches over the stem stitch. Outline the middle arch in stem stitch and cover the shape with satin stitch. Work closed herringbone stitch across the remainder of the shape and whipped stem stitch along the upper outline. Work three granitos to the right of the shape.

Beginning at the tip of the lower scroll, work palestrina stitch to the tip of the upper scroll. Stitch evenly spaced French knots along the outer edge of the scroll.

Work palestrina stitch along the outline of the remaining part of the paisley. Add a second row from the base of the mauve leaf spray to the top of the large scroll. Whip the two rows together.

Spout

Outline the paisley at the top of the spout with palestrina stitch. Embroider a granitos leaf spray inside the paisley in the same manner as before. Add three granitos to the left of the paisley. Stitch two small satin stitch leaves below the paisley. Work closed herringbone stitch across the shape below the leaves. Outline the shape in stem stitch and work a feather stitch tendril. Embroider the outline of the lower paisley in stem stitch and fill the shape with French knots. Work the lower tendril in stem stitch adding three pistil stitches at the tip. Stitch evenly spaced French knots along the tendril and along the tip of the paisley.

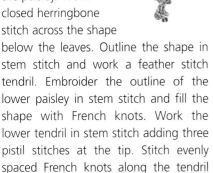

Lid

Cover the leaves in fly stitch. Embroider the tendrils among the leaves and along the lower edge of the lid in whipped stem stitch. Cover the base of the knob in satin stitch and work a row of stem stitch along the inside edge of the knob.

Handle

Embroider the tendril along the handle in whipped stem stitch.

Gold highlights

Work straight stitch highlights over all the green leaves and a straight stitch between the feather stitches. Add a gold fly stitch around the tip of each granitos. Referring to the photograph, embroider a row of stem stitch along the outline of some of the shapes to add extra highlights.

Base

Embroider a row of stem stitch around the inside edge of the base. Stitch a row of evenly spaced gold- pink beads along the upper edge.

Outlines

Using three strands of thread, embroider the teapot outlines with a row of chain stitch. Using gold, whip the chain stitch twice, whipping the second layer in the opposite direction to the first *(diag 2)*.

Diag 2

Beading

Cover any fabric showing in the teapot with closely scattered satin white beads. Secure the beading thread on the back of your work at regular intervals.

Detached elements

The flowers and leaves are embroidered on the interfacing before being cut out and attached to the main design. Cut five pieces of interfacing, each 15cm (6") square.

Flowers

Using a sharp pencil, trace five petals generously spaced onto one piece of interfacing *(diag 3)*.

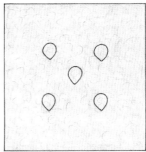

Diag 3

Embroider the five petals for one flower following the step-by-step instructions. Repeat for the remaining two flowers. Cut out the petals and set aside.

Leaves

Trace four leaves onto each of the remaining two pieces of interfacing.

For each leaf, cut an 8cm (3 ⅛") piece of green wire. Embroider the leaves in a similar manner to the petals. Work gold straight stitch highlights over each leaf. Cut out the leaves and set aside.

Tendrils

Cut a 9cm (3 ½") length of green covered wire for each tendril. Starting a short distance from one end, wrap the yarn closely around the length of wire. Leave the tails hanging free. Fold the wrapped wire in half and twist loosely together. Wrap the twisted wire around a satay stick to create the coils. Make the remaining five tendrils in the same manner.

Attaching the detached elements

Using a large yarn darner, sink the wire tails of a petal to the back at the center of a flower. Secure the wires under the position of the petal on the back of the work. Trim the excess wire and repeat

There is a great deal of poetry and fine sentiment in a chest of tea.

for the remaining four petals, overlapping the petals slightly. Attach gold-pink beads at the center of the flower. Repeat for the remaining two flowers. Attach the leaves at the marked positions in a similar manner. Attach two tendrils under the leaves on the lid and the remaining four tendrils under the leaves on the handle.

Quilting

Remove the fabric from the hoop. Place the embroidery face down on a padded surface and gently press any marks left by the hoop. Position the wadding over the wrong side of the fabric followed by the cotton lawn, aligning the edges. Ensuring the fabrics are smooth, baste the layers together. To quilt the layers, work two parallel rows of running stitch around the outlines of the teapot, beginning with the inside edge of the handle.

Turn the work over and cut a small slit in the lawn behind the teapot. Pad the teapot by pushing small amounts of fiber-fill through the slit, taking care not to over-stuff it. Stitch the opening closed.

Using the beading thread, define the shape of the teapot by working a row of tiny stab stitches along the base of the spout and the edge of the lid and base.

THREADS, BEADS & NEEDLES

Kaalund yarns 2ply silk
A = 84 pansy
B = 120 lavender
C = 148 toucan

Kaalund yarns fine 2ply wool
D = 2404 yellow
E = 2430 medium mauve
F = 2442 dk purple
G = 2470 violet
H = 2472 green

Kaalund yarns 2ply wool
I = 6473 purple

Colour Streams Silken Strands
J = Venetian sunset

Waterlilies by Caron stranded silk
K = 027 royal jewels

Thread Gatherer's Silke'n Colours
L = SNC 059 gilded lavender

Anchor stranded cotton
M = 1325 variegated mauve

Anchor stranded lamé
N = 303 gold

Anchor Marlitt stranded rayon
O = 1212 off-white

DMC stranded cotton
P = 154 dk purple (2 skeins)

DMC rayon
Q = 30915 dark fuchsia

Maria George Delica beads
R = DBR 507 metallic gold/purple iris
S = DBR 635 satin white (15gm)

Needles
No. 7 sharp
No. 7 crewel
No. 8 crewel
No. 10 beading

EMBROIDERY KEY

All embroidery is worked with one strand unless otherwise specified.

Center flower

Band = K (2 strands, stem stitch)

Outline = L (whipped stem stitch)

Stem = H (stem stitch), N (whipping)

Scallops = M (3 strands, French knot)

Small flowers = J (granitos, 8 stitches) R (beading), L (2 strands, stem stitch straight stitch)

Left hand motif

Outline = K (2 strands, palestrina stitch, whipped stem stitch)

Scroll = J (2 strands, French knot)

Center vein = L (2 strands, feather stitch, French knot)

Lower half = L (2 strands, detached chain)

Right hand motif

Filling = L (2 strands, trellis couching) R (beading)

Center vein = K (stem stitch, pistil stitch)

Outlines = E (feather stitch) L (whipped stem stitch)

Leaves = H (satin stitch)

Upper motif

Paisley = B (trellis), E (cross stitch) R (beading), I (whipped stem stitch)

Outline = A and C (palestrina stitch)

Small sprays = A (granitos, 7 stitches) D (stem stitch, detached chain)

Buds = J (granitos, 4 stitches)

Leaves = H (fly stitch, stem stitch)

Large leaf = F (stem stitch), D (closed herringbone stitch, whipped stem stitch), H (feather stitch)`

Lower left motif

Filling = Q (trellis), N (cross stitch)

Outline = L (whipped stem stitch)

Stem = C (stem stitch), N (whipping)

Tendril = A (feather stitch)

Lower center motif

Upper section = F (stem stitch, satin stitch)

Middle section = B (whipped stem stitch, seed stitch)

Lower section = H (whipped stem stitch), B (pistil stitch), H (fly stitch)

Leaves = H (fly stitch, stem stitch)

Lower right motif

Small sprays = L or M (granitos 8 stitches, stem stitch), N (fly stitch)

Right section = H (stem stitch), N (straight stitch), F (stem stitch, satin stitch), A (close herringbone stitch palestrina stitch), J (granitos, 4 stitches)

Scrolls = B (palestrina stitch) Q (2 strands, French knot)

Paisley = G (palestrina stitch whipping)

Spout

Top = C (palestrina stitch), A and J (granitos, 4 stitches), J (stem stitch)

Leaves = H (satin stitch)

Middle section = D (closed herringbone stitch, stem stitch, feather stitch) L and N (stem stitch) M (2 strands, French knot)

Tendril = L (stem stitch), B (pistil stitch) A (French knot)

Lid

Leaves = H (fly stitch)

Tendril = L (whipped stem stitch)

Top = L (satin stitch, stem stitch)

Handle

Tendril = L (whipped stem stitch)

Highlights = N (fly stitch, straight stitch, stem stitch)

Base = L (stem stitch), R (beading)

Outline = P (3 strands, chain stitch) N (double whipping)

Beading = S (beading)

Detached flowers = L (2 strands couching, blanket stitch, long and short blanket stitch), N (straight stitch) L (3 strands, French knot), R (beading)

Leaves = E (couching, long and short blanket stitch, long and short stitch) N (straight stitch)

Tendrils = H (wrapping)

Quilting = O (quilting)

PALESTRINA STITCH

Also known as old English knot, smyrna stitch, double knot stitch and tied coral stitch, palestrina stitch produces a line of raised knots useful for outlines or borders. It is important that the knots are evenly spaced and close together.

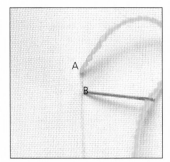

1. Bring the needle to the front at A. Take the needle to the back at B, just to the right of the line to be covered.

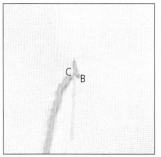

2. Bring the needle to the front at C opposite B. Pull the thread through.

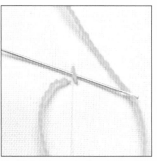

3. Slide the needle under the first stitch from right to left with the needle pointing upwards. Do not go through the fabric.

4. Begin to pull the thread through.

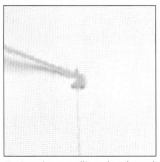

5. Continue pulling the thread through gently until the loop hugs the straight stitch.

6. Make a loop to the left.

7. Slide the needle from right to left under the thread. Emerge between B and C. Do not go through fabric. Ensure the loop is under the needle tip.

8. Gently pull the thread through forming a soft knot. **Completed first knot.**

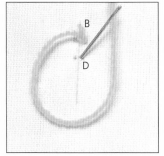

9. To begin the second stitch, take the needle to the back at D a short distance below B.

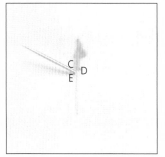

10. Bring the needle to the front at E, opposite D, and below C.

11. Complete the stitch following steps 3-8.

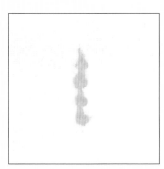

12. Continue in the same manner. End off by taking the needle to the back close to the base of the last stitch. **Completed palestrina stitch.**

DETACHED PETAL

The petals are worked on non-woven interfacing held taut in a hoop, before being cut out and attached to the main fabric.

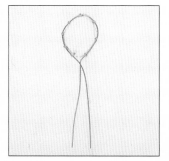 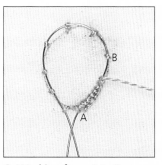 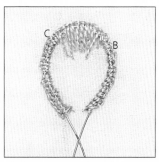 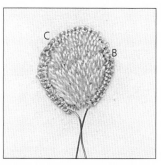

1. Cut a 7cm (2 ¾") length of beading wire and couch in place around the outline of a petal, leaving the tails overlapping at the base.

2. Working from A to B, cover the wire with closely worked blanket stitch, incorporating the couching stitches.

3. Continue in long and short blanket stitch from B to C. Cover the remaining part of the wire in blanket stitch.

4. Cover the petal with long and short stitch, working into the previous stitches between B and C.

5. Work gold straight stitch highlights over the petal. Stitch a row of evenly spaced French knots around the inside edge.

6. Carefully cut out the petal close to the blanket stitch edge. **Completed petal.**

*U*nlike the British, the French have never considered tea, which is a stimulant, suitable for children. In spite of these reservations, however, generations of little girls have received miniature tea services as a gift.

ALTERNATIVE METHOD FOR ATTACHING WIRED SHAPES

Helan's method enables you to attach the shapes without sinking the wires through the main fabric.

Petals

Place a small piece of interfacing into your hoop. Trim the wire tails close the base of each petal. Place the petals in a small circle and attach each with a few stitches at the base. Cut away the interfacing leaving a small circle under the petals.

Stitch the interfacing with the petals into position on the teapot.

Leaf and tendril

Trim the wire tails close to the base of each leaf. Position a leaf right side facing down on the interfacing and attach with a few stitches at the base of the leaf. Attach the tendril next to the base of the leaf. Fold the leaf over to the right side, concealing the raw end of the tendril.

RARE
VINTAGE

• • •

by LIZ VICKERY
of SOUTH AUSTRALIA

THE FINISHED BAG MEASURES APPROXIMATELY 15CM (6") SQUARE,
EXCLUDING THE HANDLE AND FRINGE.

Lustrous bronze silk provides a sumptuous background for the ornate decoration

on this evening bag. A pintucked lattice is accented with hundreds

of tiny sparkling beads. Bold flowers, in rich antique shades, elegantly reflect the light from their

faceted surface. Multicolored clusters surround each central intersection and a deep fringe finishes the

lower edge. A beaded gold chain forms the handle and a magnetic clasp closes the bag.

REQUIREMENTS

Fabric

30cm (12") square of pintucked antique bronze silk dupioni

30cm (12") square of antique bronze silk dupioni

30cm x 45cm wide (12" x 17 ¾") piece of shot black/gold satin

Supplies

30cm x 45cm wide (12" x 17 ¾") piece of black stiff woven interfacing eg Shapewell

5cm x 7cm wide (2" x 2 ¾") piece of acetate

30cm x 45cm wide (12" x 7 ¾") piece of black lightweight wadding, eg Pellon

Fine black beading thread

Fine white beading thread

1.5cm (⅝") gold magnetic purse clasp

5 x 6.5cm (2½") gold eye pins

8mm (⁵/₁₆") bead

30cm x 4mm (12" x ³/₁₆") antique gold chain

Round nosed jeweller's pliers

Flat edge jewelry pliers

Side snips

Tracing paper

Two-pack glue eg Araldite

Threads, Beads & Needles

See page 97.

THIS DESIGN USES

Beading · Whipping

PREPARATION FOR EMBROIDERY

Cut the interfacing in half across the width. Neaten the raw edges of the piece of pintucked silk dupioni with a machine zigzag or overlock stitch to prevent fraying. Aligning the straight grain of the fabrics, center the silk over one piece of interfacing and pin in place. Work a horizontal and a vertical row of tacking to mark the center of the design, ensuring they are placed through a row of pintucked diamonds. Note: the center of the design may not fall in the center of the fabric piece. Counting two full diamonds out from the center, tack the seam lines of the bag *(diag 1)*.

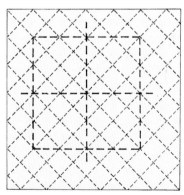

Diag 1

The bag front is cut to its exact size after the embroidery is complete.

They would talk of nothing but high life and high-lived company, with other fashionable topics,

such as pictures, taste, Shakespeare, and the musical glasses.

~ OLIVER GOLDSMITH, VICAR OF WAKEFIELD (CH. IX) ~

EMBROIDERY

See page 98 and 99 for the step-by-step instructions for the clusters and the handle.

Refer to the beading chart in the liftout sheet for the position of the beads. Refer to the embroidery key, beading chart and close-up photograph for color placement.

Use the milliner's needle for the bead embroidery and the beading needle for the fringe.

Order of work

The diamantés are glued into the bead caps at the center of each flower after the embroidery is complete.

The beaded fringe and handle are made after the bag is constructed.

Beaded pintucks

The beads along each side of the pintucks are attached with a single strand of cotton whipped into the pintuck stitches. Secure the thread under a pintuck at the top left hand corner. Take the needle under the first stitch of the pintuck inside the marked seamline and thread a satin olive Delica bead onto the needle *(diag 2)*.

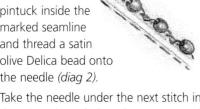

Diag 2

Take the needle under the next stitch in the pintuck and thread on a second bead. Continue to whip into the stitches of the pintucks, threading a bead onto the thread over each stitch. When reaching the end of the row, turn the fabric and repeat for the opposite side of the pintuck. Continue beading all the pintucks in this manner.

Flowers

Beaded flowers in one of two color combinations are stitched at the center of each diamond, using a doubled length of black beading thread. The color combinations are worked in alternate diagonal rows. Refer to the beading chart for placement. Starting at the top right hand diamond, secure a gold bead cap at the center of the diamond with a stitch across the cap through the filigree. Work a second stitch in the opposite direction *(diag 3)*.

Diag 3

Bring the needle to the front just above the bead cap. Thread on a 4mm ($^3/_{16}$") amethyst crystal and stitch in place pointing it towards the top of the diamond, ensuring the stitch accommodates the bead *(diag 4)*.

Diag 4

Take a second stitch through the crystal. Attach a second crystal, pointing to the base of the diamond, in the same manner as the first. Attach another four crystals evenly around the bead cap *(diag 5)*.

Diag 5

Embroider the remaining beaded flowers in this manner.

Clusters

Beaded clusters are worked at the intersections of the pintucking on alternate horizontal rows. Embroider nine beaded clusters following the step-by-step instructions, referring to the beading chart for placement.

Gold beads

Using doubled black thread, attach a gold bead at all remaining intersections of the pintucking.

CONSTRUCTION

See pages 122 and 123.

Beaded fringe

The beaded fringe is made using single black thread in the beading needle.

The drops are worked in two alternating sequences at 5mm ($^3/_{16}$") intervals along the base of the bag.

First drop

Secure the thread at one corner of the bag. Thread the beads in the following sequence:

G, C, G, B x 6, G, C, G, H, G, O, G, H, G, C, G, B x 8, G, C, G, H, G, O, G, R, K, R, G, L and G.

Ensure the bead caps surround the larger beads *(diag 6)*.

Diag 6

Take the needle over the last bead and back through the entire sequence *(diag 7)*.

Secure the thread through the seam, without ending off. Take the needle through the seam for 5mm ($^3/_{16}$") to the position of the next drop.

Second drop

Thread the beads in the following sequence:

G, C, G, B x 6, G, C, G, H, G, O, G, H, G, C, G, B x 8, G, C, G, H, G, O, G, R, J, R, G, L and G.

Diag 7

Secure the drop in the same manner as the previous drop.

Continue working the drops along the base of the bag, alternating the two sequences, finishing with the first drop sequence.

Handle

Make and attach the handle following the step-by-step instructions.

Using doubled black beading thread, stitch the last links of the handle to the bag lining through the seam allowance, 5mm ($^3/_{16}$") from the upper edge. Stitch through the seam allowance of all layers of fabric.

Finishing

Cut a small hole in a disposable cloth. Place the cloth over your work and, following the instructions on the packaging, glue the diamantés into the bead caps at the center of each flower through the hole.

Hints
ON BEADED FRINGING

1. Secure the thread firmly to the bag seam between each drop. Ensure you have enough thread in the needle to complete each drop.

2. Finish the thread by taking it back through 12 - 15 beads after securing it to the seam.

THREAD, BEADS & NEEDLES

Where numbers of beads are specified, it is advisable to purchase a few extra beads.

Anchor stranded cotton
A = 855 dk taupe

Maria George Delica beads
B = DBR 123 transparent olive gray luster (6 grams)
C = DBR 371 matte metallic olive green (1pkt)
D = DBR 671 satin olive (9 grams)

Maria George antique seed beads
E = 9102 cyclamen (1pkt)
F = 9135 pale gold (1pkt)

Czech glass hank beads size 11
G = 558 brown iris (5 grams)

Glass pearls
H = 102 x 2.5mm ($^1/_{12}$") amethyst

Czech faceted oval glass beads
I = 72 x 4mm ($^3/_{16}$") amethyst AB
J = 15 x 4mm ($^3/_{16}$") lt amethyst AB
K = 16 x 6mm ($^1/_4$") lt amethyst AB

Czech faceted oval glass drops
L = 31 x 10mm x 6mm wide ($^3/_8$" x $^1/_4$") amethyst AB

Czech multi faceted oval glass beads
M = 5 x 10mm ($^3/_8$") dk olive
N = 10 x 7mm x 5mm wide ($^5/_{16}$" x $^3/_{16}$") lt amethyst

Swarovski crystal diamond shaped roundels
O = 62 x 4mm ($^3/_{16}$") Dorado
P = 72 x 4mm ($^3/_{16}$") amethyst
Q = 108 x 3mm ($^1/_8$") lt amethyst

Filigree bead caps
R = 147 x 4mm ($^3/_{16}$") gold

Diamantés
S = 24 x 3mm ($^1/_8$") dk topaz

Needles
No. 10 beading
No. 10 milliner's

EMBROIDERY KEY

All bead embroidery is worked with a doubled length of thread unless otherwise specified.

Beaded pintucks = A and D
(1 strand, whipping, beading)
Flowers = I, P and R (beading)
S (glue to attach)
Clusters = H and R (beading)
E and Q (beading)
Gold beads = F (beading)

The sunbeams dropped
Their gold, and, passing in porch and niche,
Softened to shadows, silvery, pale, and dim,
As if the very Day paused and grew Eve.

~ SIR EDWIN ARNOLD, LIGHT OF ASIA ~

CLUSTER

The nine clusters are worked around intersections of the pintucking, using doubled white beading thread. We omitted the beading along the pintucks and used contrasting threads for photographic purposes.

1. Bring the thread to the front at W. Attach a bead cap through the filigree, inserting the needle at X.

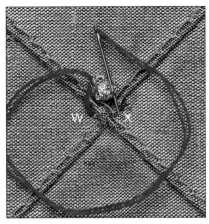

2. Re-emerge at Y. Take the needle through the filigree and thread a G onto the needle. Take the needle through the opposite side.

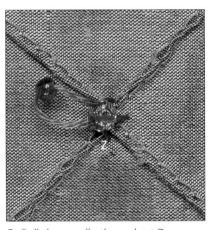

3. Pull the needle through at Z.

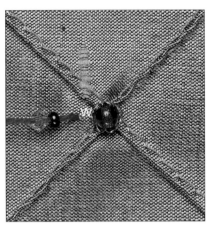

4. Re-emerge next to W. Thread E then Q onto the needle.

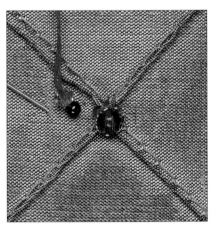

5. Take the needle to the back ensuring the stitch is long enough to accommodate the beads.

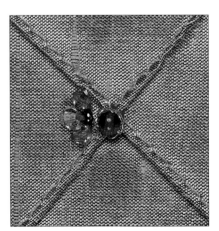

6. Take a second stitch through the beads. Attach a Q on each side of the center beads, stitching through each bead twice.

7. Repeat steps 4 - 6 for the remaining three corners.

HANDLE

The handle is made from lengths of antique gold chain and beads threaded onto eye pins.

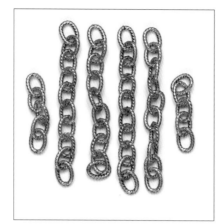

1. Using side snips, cut 4 lengths of chain each containing 10 links, and 2 lengths containing 5 links.

2. Thread beads onto an eye pin in the following sequence: R, N, R, R, M, R, R, N, R. The bead caps enclose the beads.

3. Place the 8mm ($^5/_{16}$") bead onto the eye pin. Using side snips, trim close to the bead.

4. Remove the 8mm ($^5/_{16}$") bead. Using the flat pliers, bend the wire to a right angle over the top bead cap.

5. Using the round nose pliers, turn the wire back, forming an eye without fully closing it. Bead another 4 eye pins.

6. Join the eye of one eye pin to the first link of a 5-link chain. Close the eye using round nosed pliers.

7. Gently open the eye of the opposite end and attach to a 10-link chain in the same manner.

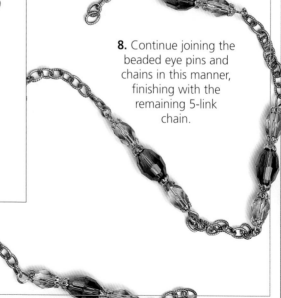

8. Continue joining the beaded eye pins and chains in this manner, finishing with the remaining 5-link chain.

KEEPSAKE

by HELEN ERIKSSON of SOUTH AUSTRALIA

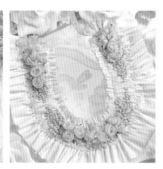

For unrivalled romance, Helen has designed a glorious matching set of a bridal bag,

horseshoe and garter. Romantic gypsophila and roses adorn the beautiful garter and horseshoe.

The soft cream and ivory shades are accentuated with dainty pearls and crystals.

The exquisite bag complements the horseshoe and garter.

Pearls and crystals highlight the silk ribbon flowers, which are worked onto purchased lace motifs.

The design of the bag is simple but effective, with elegant embroidered petals and

pearl encrusted ends on the cord.

REQUIREMENTS

Fabric

14cm x 105cm wide (5 ½" x 41 ¼") piece of cream silk dupioni for garter

14cm x 105cm wide (5 ½" x 41 ¼") piece of cream silk dupioni for horseshoe

50cm x 105cm wide (20" x 41 ¼") piece of cream silk dupioni for bag

80cm x 105cm wide (31 ½" x 41 ¼") piece of cream silk dupioni for all three items

Threads, Ribbons, Beads & Needles

See page 104.

Supplies

Beading thread eg Nymo

14cm (5 ½") square of cardboard or plastic for horseshoe

10.5cm diameter (4 ⅛") circle of cardboard or plastic for base of bag

1.5m x 7mm wide (1yd 23" x ⁵⁄₁₆") double-sided cream satin ribbon for horseshoe

40cm x 2cm wide (15 ¾" x ¾") non-roll elastic for garter

4 tea dyed guipure lace motifs each 12cm x 5cm wide (4 ¾" x 2") for bag

6 x 6mm (¼") crystal beads for base of bag

Clear nylon thread

Tracing paper

Sharp lead pencil

CONSTRUCTION

See the liftout pattern.

The garter and horseshoe are completely assembled before the embroidery is worked.

PREPARATION FOR EMBROIDERY

See the liftout pattern for the embroidery designs.

Transferring the designs

Garter

Trace the embroidery design, including the placement marks, onto tracing paper. Center the tracing over the completed garter, aligning the placement marks with the casing stitch lines. Pin in place to prevent movement. Using a large needle, pierce the tracing at the center of each rose and at the ends of the design. Dot each hole with the lead pencil. Remove the tracing.

Horseshoe

Transfer the embroidery designs to the front of the completed horseshoe in the same manner as the garter.

Bag

Trace the embroidery design and petal shaping onto the tracing paper with a black pen. Cut out the petal fronts. Place the tracing over one petal, aligning the marked petal shaping with the raw edges of the fabric. Using the lead pencil, mark the position of the lace motif and the gypsophila sprays. Repeat for the remaining three petals.

THE BAG

HORSESHOE (DETAIL)

THE GARTER

HORSESHOE (BACK)

EMBROIDERY

See page 105 for step-by-step instructions for creating the gathered ribbon roses.

Use the chenille needle when embroidering with the ribbon and the beading needle for attaching the beads. The crewel needle is used for making and securing the roses and for all other thread embroidery.

As the stitches should not be visible on the back of the garter and horseshoe, skim the needle between the fabric and elastic or cardboard. Finish off threads and ribbons on the front where they will be hidden by other embroidery or among the folds of the fabric.

The roses are made before they are attached to the fabric.

Garter

Gathered rose

Cut 18cm (7 ⅛") of both C and F and make a gathered ribbon rose following the instructions on page 105. Secure to the center dot.

Folded roses

Cut 20cm (8") of both C and G. Using the two ribbons together as if they were one, form a folded ribbon rose. Make a second rose in exactly the same manner. Attach one rose on each side of the gathered rose.

Leaves

Using the green silk ribbon, tie a knot at one end and cut off the excess tail. Bring the needle up under a rose to hide the knot. Work loop stitches around the center rose and detached chains around the side roses. Do this in a random fashion until the desired look is achieved.

Gypsophila sprays

Use the narrow cream silk ribbon to work sprays of French knots. Again, it is important not to take the needle through to the back. When starting, hide the knot among the gathers. Before pulling the needle through the French knot, bring it up at the position of the next knot, rather than to the back of the garter. Hold the knot firmly while pulling the needle through. To maintain the elasticity, do not pull the ribbon or thread too firmly as you move from one flower to the next.

Partially surround each French knot with a fly stitch for the foliage.

Crystals and pearls

Attach six crystals around the center rose. Add a cluster of three pearl beads 2cm (¾") from each end of the gypsophila sprays.

Horseshoe

Gathered roses

Make five gathered roses, securing three roses to the front of the horseshoe at the marked positions. The remaining two roses are attached to the back of the horseshoe, covering the ends of the ribbon loops.

Gathered roses

Make four gathered roses following the instructions on the opposite page. Secure a rose to each lace motif at the position shown on the photograph. Surround each rose with loop stitch leaves.

Folded roses

Make four folded roses in the same manner as the roses on the garter. Attach a rose to each lace motif at the position shown on the photograph. Surround each one with detached chain leaves.

Gypsophila sprays

Embroider the sprays of gypsophila following the garter instructions.

Crystals and pearls

Using the photograph as a guide to placement, attach pearl beads and crystals to the lace motifs except for the unattached sections at the lower edge.

Folded roses

Make twelve folded ribbon roses in the same manner as those on the garter. Attach the roses, in groups of three, at the marked positions.

Leaves

Stitch the leaves in the same manner as the leaves on the garter.

Gypsophila sprays

Work the sprays of gypsophila following the instructions for those on the garter.

Crystals and pearls

Attach pearl beads and crystals along the lower stitchline of the casing. Position the pearls at approximately 7mm ($^5/_{16}$") intervals and the crystals at approximately 3.5cm (1 $^3/_8$") intervals. Add crystals near the clusters of folded roses at the positions indicated on the design.

Bag

Lace motifs

Pin the lace motifs to the right side of the petals at the position indicated on the pattern. Using the invisible sewing thread, secure the motifs in place, leaving 2.5cm (1") at the lower end unattached.

THREADS, RIBBONS, BEADS & NEEDLES

Anchor stranded cotton
A = 858 lt fern green
B = 926 ultra lt beige

Kacoonda hand dyed silk ribbon 7mm ($^5/_{16}$") wide
C = 4 cream

Kacoonda hand dyed silk ribbon 4mm ($^3/_{16}$") wide
D = 4 cream
E = 8J lt fern green

Mokuba no.1500 organdie ribbon 11mm ($^3/_8$") wide
F = 12 cream

Mokuba no. 1500 organdie ribbon 5mm ($^3/_{16}$") wide
G = 12 cream

Beads
H = diamanté flowers 6mm ($^1/_4$") wide
I = crystal beads 4mm ($^3/_{16}$") wide
J = cream pearl beads 2mm ($^1/_{16}$") wide

Needles
No. 9 crewel
No. 13 beading
No. 20 chenille

EMBROIDERY KEY

All thread embroidery is worked with two strands.

Gathered roses
Petals = C and F (gathered ribbon rose)
B (attaching)
Center = H and J (beading)
Leaves = E (loop stitch)

Folded roses
Petals = C and G (folded ribbon rose), B (attaching)
Leaves = E (detached chain)

Gypsophila
Flowers = D (French knot, 1 wrap)
Foliage = A (fly stitch)

	GARTER	HORSESHOE	BAG
C	60cm (23 5/8")	3.4m (3yd 26")	1.6m (1yd 27")
D	1.5m (1yd 23")	3m (3yd 10")	2.5m (2yd 26")
E	1.5m (1yd 23")	3m (3yd 10")	4.5m (4yd 33 1/4")
F	20cm (8")	1m (39 1/2")	80cm (31 1/2")
G	40cm (16")	2.4m (2yd 22 1/2")	80cm (31 1/2")
H	1	7	4
I	6	17	44

- THE FINISHED BAG MEASURES 16.5CM HIGH X 14CM IN DIAMETER (6 1/2" X 5 1/2").

- THE FINISHED HORSESHOE MEASURES 17CM (6 3/4") SQUARE.

- THE GARTER MEASURES 6CM X 38CM IN CIRCUMFERENCE (2 3/8" X 15").

GATHERED RIBBON ROSE

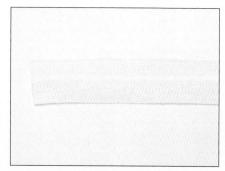

1. Cut 18cm (7") of both C and F. Place the silk ribbon on top of the organdie ribbon.

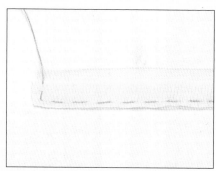

2. Stitch across one end, along one long edge and up the other end with small running stitches.

3. Pull the thread tight to gather the ribbon into a flower shape.

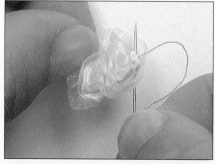

4. To hold the gathers, work two or three tiny stitches through both ends of the ribbon.

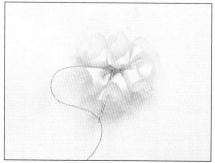

5. Attach the gathered ribbon to the fabric with tiny stitches around the center.

6. Bring the thread up through the center of the rose. Slip a flower diamanté and then a pearl bead onto the needle.

7. Take the needle back through the diamanté only.

8. Finish off with tiny back stitches in the folds of the ribbon. **Completed gathered ribbon rose.**

by CORAL MOSS
of SOUTH AUSTRALIA

PURPLE PASSION

Drawing inspiration from the timeless techniques of smocking and beading,
this fashionable evening bag creates the impression of style and opulence.
Made of silk dupion and lined with satin, the bag features a smocked and beaded insert
trimmed with piping. A covered button closes the bag on the back.

REQUIREMENTS

Fabric

30cm x 112cm wide (12" x 44") purple silk dupioni

25cm x 40cm wide (10" x 16") piece of purple satin lining

Notions

25cm x 40cm wide (10" x 16") piece of thin fusible wadding eg Pellon

90cm (35 ½") no. 0 piping cord

1 x 15mm (⅝") self cover button

Thread wax

No. 9 crewel needle (smocking)

No. 9 milliner's needle (beading)

Threads and Beads

See page 108.

PATTERN

See the liftout pattern.

We recommend you read the complete article and the liftout pattern instructions relating to this project before you begin.

The bag measures 16cm x 16.5cm wide (6 ¼" x 6 ½") and will comfortably hold essential items such as your cosmetics and mobile phone.

CUTTING OUT

See pages 125 and 126 for the cutting layouts.

Silk dupioni

Front insert: cut one, 13cm x 80cm wide (5 ⅛" x 31 ½").

Trace the pattern pieces onto light-weight interfacing or tracing paper, transferring the pattern markings. Cut out all the pieces following the instructions on page 125.

PREPARATION & PLEATING

Before pleating, neaten the raw edges of the rectangle with a zigzag or overlock stitch to prevent the silk dupioni fraying.

Pleat eleven full space rows (including two holding rows) with the top row 1.5cm (⅝") from the upper raw edge.

Unpick the pleating threads for 1.5cm (⅝") on one side. Count across 118 pleats and unpick any remaining pleats from the other side. Trim the excess fabric leaving a 1.5cm (⅝") seam allowance. Neaten the raw edge and tie off the insert so the pleated area measures 17cm (6 ¾") wide.

SMOCKING

Refer to the graph on page 108 and the step-by-step instructions on page 109 for beaded alternating cable.

Base rows

Work the cable rows first, using three strands of thread.

Begin all rows on the left hand side of the insert.

Row 1. Beginning with an over cable, work a base row of cables.

Row 2. Work a mirror image of row 1.

Rows 3 - 8. Repeat rows 1 and 2 three times.

Row 9. Repeat row 1.

Beading

Use two strands of waxed thread when smocking with the beads.

Keeping the beads clear of the seam allowances, work the picots above and below the base rows, slipping a bead onto the needle as each cable is being stitched.

CONSTRUCTION

See pages 125 - 127.

COLOR KEY

Rajmahal Art Silk

A = 115 Imperial purple

Mill Hill glass seed beads

B = 00374 rainbow (2 pkts)

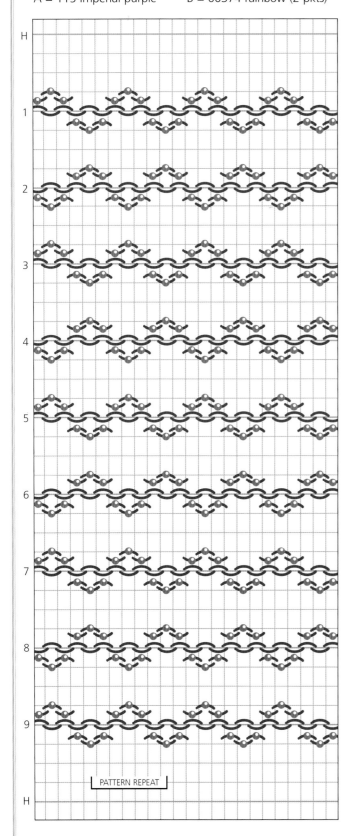

H

1

2

3

4

5

6

7

8

9

PATTERN REPEAT

H

BAGS FOR
Every Occasion

𝓔ven at the end of the 1940's, it was necessary to have a handbag of a particular style for different occasions. The well-dressed woman was expected to carry a large leather drawstring bag for use at lunchtimes, and then a teatime bag that was small and slim, big enough to hold the merest essentials.

𝓑y cocktail time, a woman's necessities would be moved into a bag that hung from the wrist, leaving her hands free to hold a glass.

𝓦hile she changed for dinner, into full evening dress, she would choose yet another bag; perhaps a little carry-all made of velvet or elegantly stitched in petit-point with a filigree silver clasp and chain.

A Century of Bags by Claire Wilcox
Quarto Publishing plc, London © 1997

Decorating with beads is an easy and effective way to add sparkle to smocking. In this project, the needle is angled differently from conventional alternating cable to allow the beads to form a more pronounced peak.

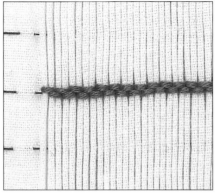

1. Base row. Using three strands of thread and beginning with an over cable, work a base row of cables.

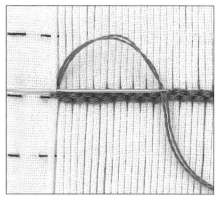

2. Beading. Using two strands of thread, bring needle to the front in the valley above the first over cable of the previous row. Take it from right to left through the first pleat.

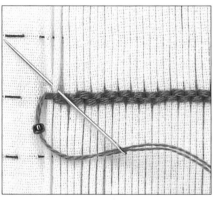

3. Pull the thread through. Slip a bead onto the needle. With the thread below and angling the needle at 45°, take it from right to left through the next pleat to the right.

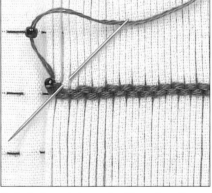

4. Pull thread through. Slip a bead onto needle. With the thread above needle, take it from right to left through next pleat to right, angling it 45° in the opposite direction.

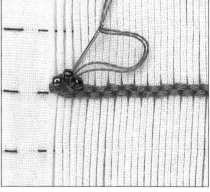

5. Pull thread through. Slip a bead onto needle. Work an under cable a needle's width above the over cable of previous row. Take needle and thread to back in valley. Work a back stitch.

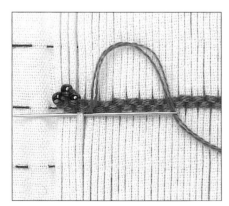

6. Bring the thread to the front in the valley below the next under cable. Take the needle back through the pleat ready to repeat the process.

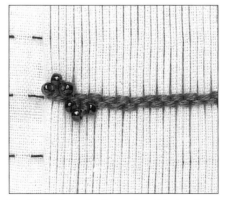

7. Pull thread through. Work three beaded cables (over, under, over). On last cable, take the needle to the back and secure the thread as before.

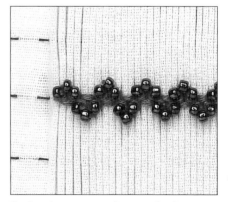

8. Continue across the row in the same manner. **Completed beaded alternating cable.**

PEARLS OF WISDOM

*For color photos and full details
see pages 10 - 13*

Attaching the ribbons

Cut four lengths of ribbon each 1m (40″) long. Cut one end of each ribbon at an angle *(diag 1)*.

Neaten the angled end with a small amount of Fray Check and allow to dry.

ribbon

remove excess

Diag 1

Beginning 3cm (1 ¼″) away from the heel on each side, unpick the stitching on the binding tape around the upper edge of the slipper, leaving an opening of 5cm (2″) *(diag 2)*.

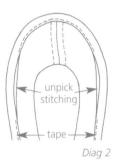

unpick stitching

tape

Diag 2

Position one length of ribbon with the neatened edge against the inside of the upper edge of the slipper *(diag 3)*. Tack to hold in place.

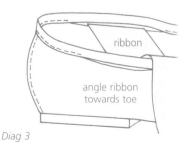

ribbon

angle ribbon towards toe

Diag 3

Reposition the binding tape over the side of the slipper, concealing the end of the ribbon and restitch in place through all layers *(diag 4)*. Repeat for the remaining side of the slipper.

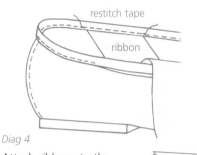

restitch tape

ribbon

Diag 4

Attach ribbons to the second slipper in the same manner as the first.

Fold the remaining raw ends of the ribbons in half and cut to form a V *(diag 5)*.

Apply Fray Check to the cut ends and allow to dry.

selvedges

fold

Diag 5

● ● ●

DARE TO DREAM

*For color photos and full details
see pages 14 - 17*

CUTTING OUT

Ivory silk dupioni

Front: cut one, 31.6cm (12 ½″) square
Button cover: cut one, 5cm (2″) square

Blush pink silk dupioni

Back: cut one the same size as the front after the pintucks are stitched.

Button cover: cut one, 5cm (2″) square
Frill: cut two, each 26cm x 135cm wide (10¼″ x 53″)

CUTTING LAYOUT

Blush pink silk dupioni

1. Back
2. Button cover
3. Frill

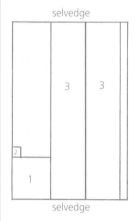

selvedge

3   3

2

1

selvedge

CONSTRUCTION

Seam allowances are 1cm (⅜″) unless otherwise specified. The shaded areas on the following diagrams indicate the right side of the fabric.

1. Preparation

Remove all traces of the fabric marker by rinsing the embroidered front in cold running water. Leave until dry. Place the embroidery, face down on a well padded surface and press.

2. Piping the front

Matching raw edges and beginning near the middle on one side, pin the piping to the right side of the front. Position the piping so the corded edge lies just below the intersection of the row of partial diamonds *(diag 1)*.

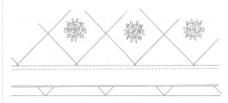

Diag 1

Clip the piping heading so it can curve around the corners. Overlap the ends of the piping at the beginning and curve them into the seam allowance *(diag 2)*.

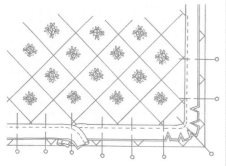

Diag 2

Stitch along the piping stitch line.

3. Making the frill

With right sides facing, stitch the ends of the strips together to form a circle. Press the seams open.

With wrong sides together, fold the frill in half along the length *(diag 3)*. Press.

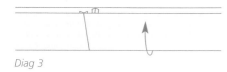

Diag 3

Using the seams as two quarter marks, measure and mark the frill into quarters at the raw edge with the water-soluble fabric marker.

Beginning at one seam and stitching through both layers, stitch two rows of gathering around the raw edges on half of the frill *(diag 4)*.

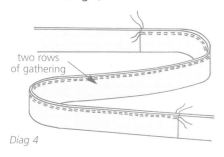

two rows of gathering

Diag 4

Repeat for the remaining half .

4. Attaching the frill

Using the fabric marker, mark the midpoint on each side of the cushion front at the raw edge *(diag 5)*.

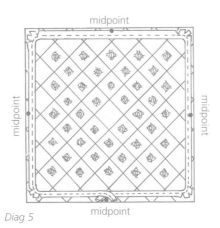

midpoint

midpoint

midpoint

midpoint

Diag 5

Matching quarter marks and the stitch-line of the frill with the stitchline of the piping, pin the frill to the front. Pull up the gathers to fit. Distribute the gathers evenly along the sides, allowing extra fullness at the corners *(diag 6)*.

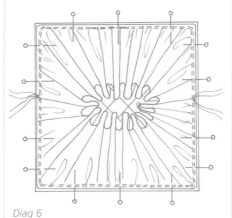

Diag 6

Tack the frill in place. With the wrong side of the front facing up, stitch around all sides along the previous stitchline.

5. Finishing the beading

Following the instructions on page 16, attach clusters of three beads to the remaining intersections of the pintucked diamonds. Take care not to catch the seam allowance.

6. Joining the front to the back

With right sides together, pin the front to the back. The piping and frill are sandwiched between. Leaving a 15cm (6") opening on one side and with the front facing up, stitch around all sides between the previous line of stitching and the corded edge of the piping *(diag 7)*.

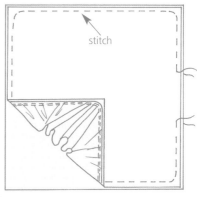

stitch

Diag 7

Trim the seam and clip the corners. Turn the cushion through to the right side and press. Press under the seam allowances along the opening.

7. Filling the cushion

Fill the cushion with the polyester fiber-fill until it is the desired plumpness. Ensure it is pushed well into the corners. Hand stitch the opening closed.

8. Covering the buttons

Cover one button with the blush pink fabric and the remaining button with the ivory fabric. Following the step-by-step instructions on page 17, cover the ivory button with seed beads.

9. Attaching the buttons

Use the doll needle and a 50cm (19 ¾") length of thread, made up of six strands of C. Take the needle through the center back of the cushion and emerge in the middle of the center diamond on the front. Leave a 20cm (8") tail of thread on the back. Take the thread through the shank of the beaded button and to the back of the cushion *(diag 8)*.

Diag 8

Pull the threads until the button is snug into the cushion. Tie the threads into a firm knot.

Pass each tail of thread in opposite directions through the shank of the pink button (diag 9).

Diag 9

Thread one tail into the needle and take it through the cushion, emerging beneath the beaded button. Repeat with the remaining tail. Pull the tails of thread firmly and tie into a secure knot (diag 10).

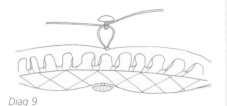

Diag 10

Re-thread the tails into the needle. Take the thread into the cushion and re-emerge on the back. Pull the thread firmly and cut it close to the cushion. The ends will retract into the cushion.

NOSTALGIA

*For color photos and full details
see pages 18 - 25*

ALTERING THE PATTERN

Use the following method if your chosen purse frame is different from the original.

1. Making the template

Using tracing paper, trace the shape of the purse frame. Exclude the sewing holes on the lower edge and the hinges.

Mark the center at the clasp. Transfer the shape onto cardboard and cut out (diag 1).

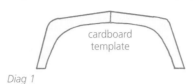

cardboard template

Diag 1

2. Marking the new shape

Using the pattern provided, trace all lines excluding the upper curved stitchline and cutting line. Rule a line joining the dots which indicate the gathering positions. Place the cardboard template onto the traced pattern with the inner edge of one end aligned with one dot. Position the remaining curved end along the ruled line. Beginning at the dot and ending at the marked center, trace the lower curved line of the template (diag 2).

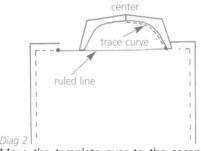

center

trace curve

ruled line

Diag 2

Move the template over to the second side and repeat the process. Remove the template. Blend the curved lines together at the center. This now becomes the new stitchline.

Measure and mark a 1cm (³⁄₈") seam allowance above the new stitchline. Cut out the pattern following the new marked cutting line (diag 3).

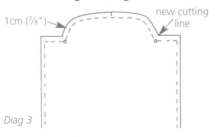

1cm (³⁄₈")

new cutting line

Diag 3

CUTTING OUT

Trace the pattern piece and all markings onto lightweight interfacing or tracing paper. Cut out the purse shape from the silk and the lining, transferring the

markings. With the water-soluble fabric marker, mark the front of the silk at the positions for the top and bottom of the embroidery design with small dots. Aligning the scalloped edge of the lace with the marking on the pattern, cut out the lace for the front overlay to the shaded area.

CONSTRUCTION

All seam allowances are 1cm (³⁄₈") unless otherwise specified. The shaded areas on the following diagrams indicate the right side of the fabric.

1. Joining the front to the back

Fold the silk along the beaded foldline with right sides together. Ensuring the strings of beads are out of the way, pin the front to the back at the sides. The lace is sandwiched between the layers. Stitch the side seams (diag 1).

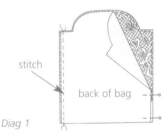

stitch

back of bag

Diag 1

Turn to the right side and press. With right sides together, stitch the sides of the lining in the same manner. Press the seam, leaving the lining inside out.

2. Completing the beading

At the two lower corners of the purse, stitch the remaining beads in place (diag 2).

Diag 2

3. Gathering the top

Beginning and ending at the dots at the base of the curve, stitch two rows of machine gathering along the top edge of the front. Place the first row of gathering on the stitchline and the second row 3mm (⅛") away within the seam allowance (diag 3).

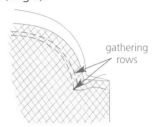

Diag 3

Work gathering across the back in the same manner. Beginning and ending at the dots, stitch two rows of machine gathering along the straight edges at the sides (diag 4).

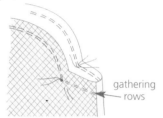

Diag 4

Repeat for the lining.

4. Attaching the purse frame

Keeping the gathering threads out of the way, clip the seam allowance up to the dots at the base of the curves. Press under 1cm (⅜") around the curved raw edges of the purse and along the straight edges at the sides. Pull up the gathering threads on the front to measure approximately 18cm (7") on the curve between the dots. Repeat for the back and the lining. Open the purse frame out flat. Matching centers and aligning the dots at the base of the curves on the front of the purse with the first hole in the frame, handstitch the gathered edge to the frame. Take one stitch into each hole of the frame using a stabbing motion and adjusting the gathers as you work (diag 5).

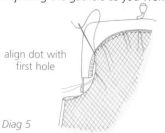

align dot with first hole

Diag 5

Repeat for the back of the purse.

5. Attaching the lining

Place the lining inside the purse with the wrong side of the lining facing the wrong side of the silk. Using the same method as the silk, attach the lining to the inside edge of the purse frame.

Using the gathering threads at the sides, pull up the slack of silk and lining fabric so that they fit snugly over the hinges. Tie off the gathering threads and trim to 4cm (1 ½"). Push the tails between the silk and lining. Ensuring the raw edges are turned under, handstitch the silk to the lining along the folded edges (diag 6).

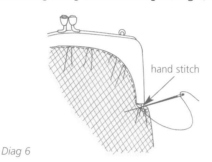

hand stitch

Diag 6

6. Finishing

Fold under 6mm (¼") at the raw end of the braid. Using a blind stitch, stitch the top edge of the braid trim to the outside of the purse below the curved edge of the frame front. Ensure the previous handstitches and the gathered edge of the silk and lace is covered (diag 7).

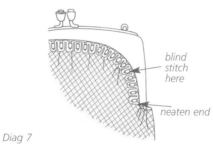

blind stitch here

neaten end

Diag 7

At the other end of the frame cut the braid allowing 6mm (¼") to extend beyond the last hole. Fold under to neaten as before. Blind stitch the lower edge of the braid to the purse in the same manner. Repeat on the back of the purse. Using the same method, attach braid to the inside of the purse. Attach the chain to the frame with jewelry pliers.

SILKEN TOUCH

For color photos and full details see pages 26 - 29

CUTTING OUT

Pink silk dupioni

Cut four rectangles, each 15cm x 22cm wide (6" x 9"). After the embroidered areas have been worked, cut out the strawberries along the marked cutting lines.

CUTTING LAYOUT

Blue silk dupioni

1. Large strawberry

Pink silk dupioni

1. Large strawberry
2. Small strawberry

CONSTRUCTION

All seam allowances are 1cm (⅜") unless otherwise specified. The shaded areas on the following diagrams indicate the right side of the fabric.

1. Seam

With right sides together and raw edges even, pin the two straight edges together (diag 1).

tack

Diag 1

Stitch. Stitch again over the previous stitchline and trim the seam to 6mm (¼") and clip the tip. Turn to the right side. Complete any embroidery on the seam.

2. Shaping the top

Diag 2

Stitch a row of gathering around the top of the opening, along the stitchline *(diag 2)*.

Fill the strawberry firmly with fiber-fill, pulling the gathering thread as the filling is inserted.

Diag 3

Insert the knotted end of the twisted cord into the opening and pull up the gathering threads firmly *(diag 3)*.

Insert the gathering thread into a needle and handstitch the opening closed, working several stitches through the base of the cord to secure *(diag 4)*.

Diag 4

3. Attaching the frill

Handstitch a row of gathering along one long edge of the silk ribbon for the rose, crystal and pansy strawberries *(diag 5)*.

Diag 5

For the rosebud strawberry, fold the ribbon in half along the length and press. Handstitch a row of gathering close to the foldline *(diag 6)*.

Diag 6

Pull up the gathers firmly. Starting at the seam of the strawberry, begin stitching the ribbon to the top around the twisted cord *(diag 7)*.

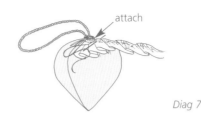

Diag 7

When reaching the seam again, secure the thread and end off, taking the needle through the strawberry and re-emerging on the outside. Cut off the excess thread. The tail will spring back and be hidden inside the strawberry.

● ● ●

GLAD TIDINGS

For color photos and full details see pages 30 - 33

CUTTING LAYOUTS

Pale ivory silk dupioni

1. Front patchwork piece

3. Front patchwork piece

5. Back

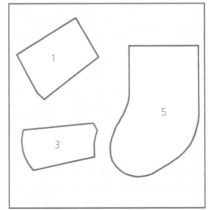

Ivory silk dupioni

2. Front patchwork piece

4. Front patchwork piece

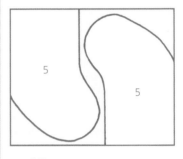

Cream silk broadcloth

5. Front and back lining

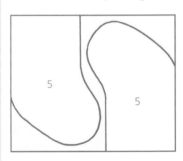

Wadding

5. Front and back padding

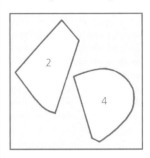

CONSTRUCTION

All seam allowances are 1cm (³⁄₈") unless otherwise specified. The shaded areas on the following diagrams indicate the right side of the fabric.

1. Preparing the front

Pin the remaining piece of wadding to the wrong side of the front.

2. Joining the front to the back

With right sides together, pin the front to the back at the sides and around the foot. Stitch, leaving the upper edge open. Remove the basting stitches.

Trim the wadding close to the stitching. Trim the seam and clip the curves.

3. Making the lining

With right sides together, join the two lining pieces, leaving the upper edge open and leaving a 6cm (2 ½") opening on the lower edge of the foot (diag 1). Turn to the right side.

leave open

Diag 1

With right sides together, slip the lining into the stocking and stitch around the upper edge, matching side seams (diag 2).

stitch

Diag 2

Turn out through the opening in the lining and handstitch the opening closed.

Push the lining down into the stocking. Baste the upper edge. Where necessary, add any beads near the seams.

4. Attaching the gold wire trim

Starting at the left hand seam and stitching from left to right, couch the wire in place with invisible thread, stitching between the loops. Overlap the ends and couch to secure.

5. Making the twisted cord

Cut 15 lengths of C, each 1.2m (48") long. Fold in half and knot the cut ends together.

Hook the loop of the folded end over a cup hook or door handle. Slide a pencil through the knotted end. Keeping the threads taut, twist them with the pencil in a clockwise direction until the twist has the desired tension (diag 3).

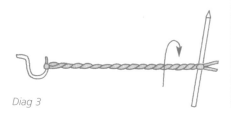

Diag 3

Still keeping them taut, fold the threads in half, holding at the halfway point (diag 4).

Diag 4

Release in short sections until all the cord is twisted (diag 5).

Diag 5

Remove the knotted end from the doorknob. Knot the cord 3cm (1 ¼") from each end (diag 6).

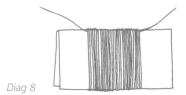

Diag 6

6. Making the tassels

Fold a 3cm x 6.5cm wide (1 ¼" x 2 ½") piece of cardboard in half. Wind C around the cardboard 150 times (diag 7).

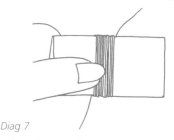

Diag 7

Using the chenille needle and a strand of moistened quilting thread, slide under the gold threads on the folded edge of the cardboard (diag 8).

Diag 8

Slide sharp scissors between the two layers of cardboard at the unfolded end. Cut through all the loops of the thread.

With the threads on top, carefully open out the cardboard. Lay the knot of one end of the twisted cord onto the threads. Position the knot just below the fold (diag 9).

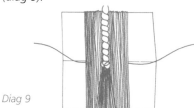

Diag 9

Carefully lift the ends of the quilting thread, pulling the cut threads up to evenly wrap around the cord. Tie in a very firm knot just above the knot in the cord. Pull tightly and knot the thread again (diag 10).

tie here

Diag 10

Fold the threads down over the knot (diag 11).

Thread 50cm (20") of C in a chenille needle and wrap to create a band of threads just below the knot to form the neck of the tassel (diag 12).

Diag 11

Diag 12

Secure with three blanket stitches. Pass the needle to the inside of the tassel skirt and emerge at the base. Pull to sink the blanket stitches. Cut the thread off level with the base.

Repeat for the second tassel.

Trim the tassels.

7. Attaching the bow

Tie the cord in a bow around a glass to make a hanging loop in the middle (*diag 13*).

Diag 13

Attach the bow securely to the upper edge of the stocking at the back seam.

ANTIQUE GOLD

For color photos and full details see pages 34 - 39

CUTTING LAYOUTS

Cream moiré fabric

1. Bag front & back

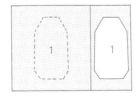

Silk dupioni fabric & Pellon wadding

1. Lining front and back, wadding front and back.

CONSTRUCTION

All seam allowances are 1cm (3/8") unless otherwise specified. The shading on the following diagrams indicates the right side of the fabric.

1. Preparing the frame

We have blackened our handle to give an antique look. If you wish to do the same, make sure you work in a clear space away from your embroidery. Paint the handle inside and out with black craft paint. Leaving the paint in the grooves of the frame, rub over wiith a tissue or cotton wool. Spray to seal the frame inside and out with a clear varnish suitable for using on metal. Wait until completely dry before attaching to the bag.

2. Joining the front to the back

With right sides together, pin and tack the front and back pieces around the outside edges between the dots. Stitch, leaving the top open (*diag 1*). Do not turn through.

moiré

stitch

Diag 1

3. Joining the lining

Tack a piece of the wadding to the wrong side of each lining piece. With lining right sides together, pin and tack around the outside edges between the dots.

lining & wadding

stitch

Diag 2

Stitch in the same manner as the moiré fabric leaving an 8cm (3 1/8") opening along the lower edge (*diag 2*). Turn through to the right side.

4. Joining the top edges

Insert the lining into the bag with right sides together.

Match the seams at the dots where the previous stitching finishes. On one side pin and tack the bag and lining together along the top edge. Stitch, beginning and ending at the dots (*diag 3*).

stitch

moiré

Diag 3

Repeat for the remaining side. Clip the seams at the dots and trim the corners (*diag 4*).

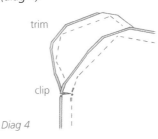

trim

clip

Diag 4

Turn the bag to the right side through the opening in the lining. Turn under and press the seam allowances along the opening. Stitch along the edge to close the opening (*diag 5*).

stitch

Diag 5

Push the lining into the bag.

Carefully roll out the top edges of the bag and lining, and press to ensure the seam lies along the top.

5. Attaching the frame

Open the frame and align the side seams to each hinge. Tack in place on either side of each hinge (*diag 6*).

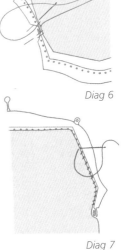

Diag 6

Place the edge of the bag to cover the holes in the frame. Handstitch the bag in place, taking one stitch into each hole, using a stabbing motion (*diag 7*).

Diag 7

6. Finishing

Handstitch the gold cord around the bag on the seamline. Leave a tail of 1cm (3/8") on each end and wrap with thread to prevent unraveling. Fold under 6mm (1/4") at the raw end of the braid.

Beginning at one hinge, place the folded end over one of the tails of gold cord. Handstitch the braid trim around the top edge of the bag. At the second hinge enclose the remaining tail of gold cord as you attach the braid. On meeting the start of the braid, trim any excess and turn under 6mm (¼") at the end. Complete stitching *(diag 8).*

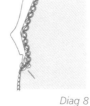

Diag 8

7. Fringe

See page 37 for instructions for working the fringe.

8. Handle

Attach a split ring to one side of the frame. Thread one end of the length of gold plait through the split ring and fold up for 5cm (2"). Starting 1.5cm (⅝") away from the split ring, bind the end to the long piece for 1cm (⅜") by wrapping one strand of the gold metallic thread around both pieces *(diag 9).*

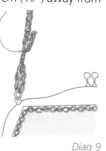

Diag 9

As you near completion, trim the short end so that it will sit just under the end of the wrapping. The plait unravels very easily and trimming as you are finishing the wrapping makes it easier to work with. End off securely with several back stitches, taking the tail back through the wrapping. Repeat for the remaining end of the handle.

BERRY DELIGHT

For color photos and full details see pages 40 - 47

CONSTRUCTION

Arranging the berries

Using the photographs as a guide, place the berries onto the embroidered foliage and stitch in place. Attach the large berries first, followed by the small berries and currants.

Inserting the fabric into the lid

Carefully remove the running stitch from around the design.

Follow the manufacturer's instructions for assembling the lid.

Design 1 requires:
1 small strawberry
1 large blackberry
1 small blackberry
2 blueberries
2 mulberries
2 red currants

Design 2 requires:
1 large strawberry
2 small strawberries

Design 3 requires:
2 small blackberries
3 red currants
3 blueberries
scattered beads

Design 4 requires:
1 large blackberry
1 small blackberry
1 mulberry
3 red currants
3 blueberries

WINTER LOVE

For color photos and full details see pages 52 - 59

CUTTING OUT

Where pattern pieces are not provided, cut the pieces according to the measurements below.

Antique gold silk dupioni

Back: cut two, each 32cm x 17.5cm wide (12 ⅝" x 6 ⅞")

Appliqué piece: cut one, 10cm (4") square

Bias strip for piping: cut three, each 50cm x 3cm wide (19 ¾" x 1 ¼")

Quilter's muslin

Cushion insert: cut two, each 40cm (15 ¾") square

CUTTING LAYOUTS

Off-white cotton

1. Embroidered panel

Claret silk dupioni

2. Border

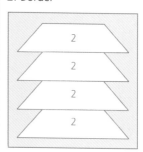

Antique gold silk dupioni

3. Back

4. Appliqué piece

5. Bias strip for piping

Quilter's muslin

6. Insert

CONSTRUCTION

All seam allowances are 1cm ($^3/_8$") unless otherwise specified. The shaded areas in the following diagrams indicate the right side of the fabric.

1. Preparing the front

Place the embroidered panel face down on a well padded surface. Carefully press the fabric. Cut to size along the marked cutting lines.

2. Forming the mitered border

With right sides facing and matching raw edges, place the first piece of the border over the second piece and pin along the diagonal corner.

Stitch from the outer edge to the inner edge stitchline, reinforcing the stitching at the marked point (diag 1).

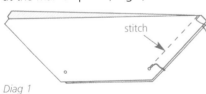

Diag 1

Press the seam open. Repeat for the remaining three corners, creating a frame (diag 2).

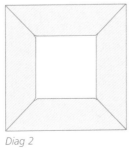

Diag 2

3. Attaching the border

With right sides facing and matching raw edges, place one inner edge of the border along one side of the embroidered panel, matching the marked points.

Stitch along the inner edge of the border between the marked points (diag 3).

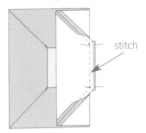

Diag 3

Repeat for the remaining three sides. Press the seams towards the border (diag 4).

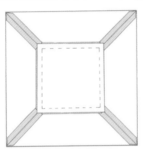

Diag 4

4. Making the piping

With right sides together, place one end of the first bias strip at a right angle over the end of a second piece. Pin and stitch. Repeat for the remaining strip to form one long strip. Press the seams open.

Place the piping cord along the center of the bias strip on the wrong side. Fold the fabric over the cord and pin. Using a zipper foot, stitch close to the cord (diag 5).

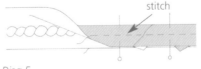

Diag 5

5. Attaching the piping

Leaving a 5cm (2") tail, begin with the piping at the center of the lower edge of the cushion front.

With right sides together and matching raw edges, pin the piping to the border.

When reaching the first corner clip the piping heading into the corner point (diag 6).

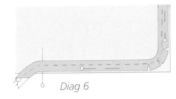

Diag 6

Continue pinning the piping in the same manner until reaching the starting point. Allowing a 5cm (2") tail to overlap, trim any excess length of piping.

Lay the ends of the piping side by side and mark each with a pin at the center point.

Unpick the stitching on the piping for 4cm (1 $^1/_2$") away from the pin marks on both ends (diag 7).

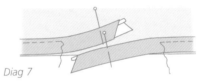

Diag 7

Uncover the piping cord back to the stitching on both ends. Wrap sewing thread around the cord for approximately 6mm ($^1/_4$"), beginning at the center point at each end (diag 8).

Diag 8

Trim away the excess length of piping cord on both ends (diag 9).

Diag 9

Open out the ends of the bias strips and measure a 1cm ($^3/_8$") seam allowance beyond the pin marks. Cutting along the straight grain (diagonally across the strip) trim away the excess lengths of fabric (diag 10).

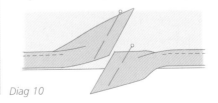

Diag 10

With right sides together, place one end at right angles over the other end. Stitch along the stitchline *(diag 11)*.

Diag 11

Press the seam open. With the cord ends butting each other, refold the bias strip over the cord and restitch *(diag 12)*. Stitch along the piping stitchline.

Diag 12

6. Joining the back pieces

Neaten one long side of each back piece. Press under a 1.5cm (⅝") seam allowance along the neatened edge on each piece. Unfold.

Matching the pressed foldlines, place the two pieces right sides together. At each end, stitch along the foldline for 6cm (2 ⅜"). Tack along the remainder of the foldline *(diag 13)*. Press the seam open.

tack here

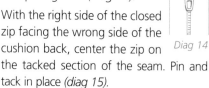

Diag 13

7. Inserting the zip

Stitch a bartack across the top of the zip to hold the two pieces of tape together *(diag 14)*.

With the right side of the closed zip facing the wrong side of the cushion back, center the zip on the tacked section of the seam. Pin and tack in place *(diag 15)*.

Diag 14

tack

Diag 15

With the right side facing up, stitch the zip in place, stitching 6mm (¼") from the seam on both sides and across the ends *(diag 16)*.

Remove the tacking and open the zip.

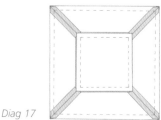

stitch

Diag 16

8. Joining the front to the back

With right sides together and matching raw edges, pin and tack the cushion front to the back. The piping is sandwiched between. With the wrong side of the front facing up, stitch around all sides along the previous stitchline *(diag 17)*.

Turn through to the right side and press.

Diag 17

9. Cushion insert

Place the two pieces of quilter's muslin together and stitch around all four sides leaving a 15cm (6") opening along one side *(diag 18)*.

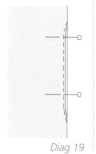

Diag 18

Turn to the right side and fill with fiber-fill. Pin the opening closed and topstitch close to the edge *(diag 19)*.

Place the cushion insert inside the cover.

Diag 19

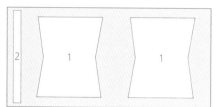

CAPRICE

For color photos and full details see pages 64 - 73

CUTTING OUT

Where pattern pieces are not provided, cut the pieces according to the measurements below.

Black silk dupioni

Cut one piece, 37cm x 3cm wide (14 ½" x 1 ¼") for the handle

Interfacing

Cut one piece, 37cm x 3cm wide (14 ½" x 1 ¼") for the handle

CUTTING LAYOUTS

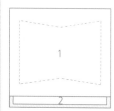

Black silk dupioni

1. Bag
2. Handle

Aubergine satin

1. Lining

Fusible interfacing

1. Bag & lining
2. Handle

CONSTRUCTION

All seam allowances are 1cm (³⁄₈") unless otherwise specified. The shaded areas on the following diagrams indicate the right side of the fabric.

1. Preparing the fabric

Cut out the embroidered bag along the marked cutting lines. Fuse the piece of interfacing to the wrong side of the satin. Using the pattern provided, cut out the lining.

2. Constructing the bag

With right sides together and matching raw edges, pin the front to the back at the sides. Stitch (diag 1).

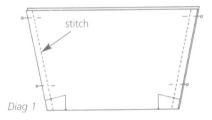

Diag 1

Press the seams open.

Bring the side seam and the marked point on the base together.

Pin and stitch across the end of the base along the marked line (diag 2). Repeat for the remaining end.

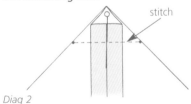

Diag 2

3. Constructing the base

Round the corners of the template plastic with scissors. At each corner, pierce two small holes with a needle at the marked positions. Place the plastic into the base of the bag and fold the corners over the top (diag 3).

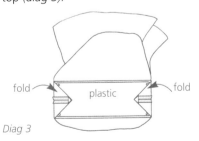

Diag 3

Stitch the plastic onto the bag base through the holes with strong black thread (diag 4). Turn to the right side.

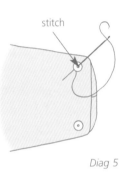

Diag 4

4. Feet

Using a single strand of M and leaving a long tail at the beginning and the end, wrap four pebble beads in the same manner as the berries.

Thread both ends through a needle and securely stitch each bead in place at a corner of the base through the holes in the plastic (diag 5).

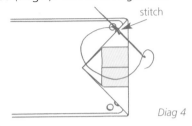

Diag 5

5. Lining

Construct the lining in the same manner as the bag, omitting the plastic. Do not turn to the right side.

Attach the frame to the bag following the step-by-step instructions on pages 72 - 73.

6. Making and attaching the handle

Fuse the interfacing to the wrong side of the silk piece. Fold the strip in half along its length and press. Open out the fabric. Turn in 6mm (¼") at each end and press (diag 6).

Diag 6

Fold each long raw edge to the foldline and press (diag 7).

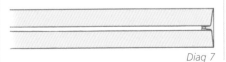

Diag 7

Refold, bringing the two folded edges together. Machine stitch along both sides of the handle (diag 8).

Diag 8

Push one end of the handle through a frame loop. Fold 1cm (³⁄₈") around the loop and, using matching thread, stitch the end to the handle (diag 9). Repeat for the remaining end.

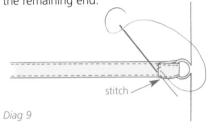

Diag 9

REJOICE

For color photos and full details see pages 74 - 83

CONSTRUCTION

All seam allowances are 1cm (³⁄₈") unless otherwise specified. The shaded areas on the following diagrams indicate the right side of the fabric.

1. Preparing the embroidered piece

Place the embroidery, right side down, on a well padded surface and pin in place along all sides (diag 1).

Diag 1

Steam and leave to dry. Cut the pieces to the exact size along the marked cutting lines.

2. Twisted cord

Cut six 90cm (35 ½") lengths of E. Refer to Glad Tidings construction, step 5 on page 115 for making the twisted cord.

3. Tassel

Cut the piece of card in half across the width and place the pieces together (diag 2).

Diag 2

Fold in half. Cut a 30cm (12") length of silk thread and set aside. Wind the remaining silk around the card. Thread two 30cm (12") lengths of quilting thread into the tapestry needle. Slide the needle under the wrapped threads at the top of the card.

Tie the quilting thread around the bundle of threads in a very tight knot. Using sharp scissors, cut the wrapped threads between the lower edges of the card (diag 3).

Diag 3

Remove the card and smooth the tassel threads, leaving the quilting threads free at the top.

Wrap the length of silk three times tightly around the thread bundle, 1cm (⅜") from the top, to form the neck.

To secure, thread one tail into the tapestry needle and work two blanket stitches around the wrapped threads. Finish off by passing each thread down through the tassel and trim level with the skirt. Repeat for the second tail (diag 4).

thread through

Diag 4

Thread a 30cm (12") length of E into the tapestry needle and knot the end. Take the needle into the tassel just below the neck and re-emerge above the neck to sink the knot into the tassel.

Wrap the gold thread smoothly around the neck to create a 5mm (³⁄₁₆") wide band. Pass the needle through the tassel a couple of times below the neck to secure the thread. Pull taut and snip.

To trim the tassel, cut a piece of tissue paper measuring 5cm x 7.5cm wide (2" x 3"). Rule a line 5mm (³⁄₁₆") from the lower edge. Carefully comb the tassel skirt ensuring all the threads are straight.

Place the tassel on the unmarked side of the paper aligning the neck with the top edge. Roll the tassel into the paper very tightly (diag 5).

roll tightly

Diag 5

Using very sharp scissors, cut along the marked line to trim the skirt (diag 6).

3. Constructing the bell

Staystitch along the stitchline on the lower edge of each piece (diag 7).

Diag 6

Fold the twisted cord in half and place over the center top of the back bell piece on the right side, aligning the cut ends with the raw edge of the fabric. Stitch securely in place (diag 8).

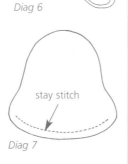

stay stitch

Diag 7

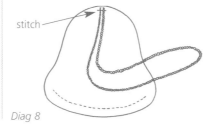

stitch

Diag 8

Position the front piece over the back with right sides together and matching raw edges, sandwiching the cord between.

Pin and stitch, leaving an opening along the base, between the marked positions (diag 9).

stitch

leave open

Diag 9

Clip the curves and turn to the right side through the opening.

4. Attaching the tassel

Thread the thread tails at the top of the tassel into the no. 4 needle. Thread on the cream metallic crystal, round gold spacer, square crystal, round spacer, large crystal and bell-cap (diag 10).

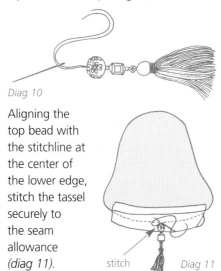

Diag 10

Aligning the top bead with the stitchline at the center of the lower edge, stitch the tassel securely to the seam allowance (diag 11).

stitch

Diag 11

Fill the bell firmly with fiber-fill. Fold the seam allowance to the inside of the opening and stitch the opening closed using ladder stitch.

5. Finishing

With the right side of the bell facing, work Armenian edging stitch along the lower edge of the bell, following the step-by-step instructions on page 79.

RARE VINTAGE

*For color photos and full details
see pages 92 - 99*

CUTTING OUT

Cut the embroidered piece to the exact size, 1cm (³⁄₈") from the tacked stitch lines *(diag 1)*.

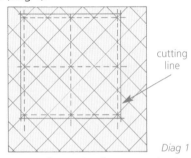

cutting line

Diag 1

Referring to the cutting layouts and using the front piece as a template, cut the back from the antique bronze silk dupioni.

Cut the remaining pieces for the lining, interfacing and wadding in the same manner.

CUTTING LAYOUTS

Antique bronze silk dupioni

1. Back

Shot black/gold satin and black lightweight wadding

1. Front and back lining and interlining

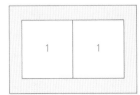

Black interfacing

1. Front and back

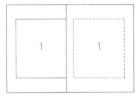

CONSTRUCTION

All seam allowances are 1cm (³⁄₈") unless otherwise specified. The shaded areas on the following diagrams indicate the right side of the fabric.

Note: use a zipper foot when stitching the beaded fabric to avoid chipping the beads.

1. Constructing the bag

Center the beaded bag front over one piece of wadding. Tack in place along all sides. Center the remaining piece of interfacing over the second piece of wadding. Center the bag back over the interfacing and tack along all sides.

With the right sides together and matching raw edges, position the front piece over the back.

Pin and stitch along the sides and base, pivoting the needle at the corners *(diag 2)*.

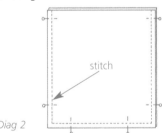

stitch

Diag 2

Trim the interfacing and wadding close to the stitchline. Fold the seam allowance of the silk over at the corners and press gently *(diag 3)*. Turn the bag to the right side.

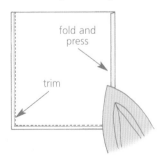

fold and press

trim

Diag 3

2. Preparing the lining

On each lining piece, find the center of the top edge and measure down 3.5cm (1 ³⁄₈"). Mark the positions for the prongs of the purse snap 1cm (³⁄₈") apart *(diag 4)*.

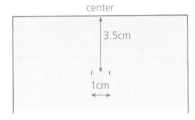

center

3.5cm

1cm

Diag 4

Using very sharp, pointed scissors, cut a very small slit through the lining at the marked positions. Cut the piece of acetate in half across the width. Make two small slits to correspond with the slits in the lining. Undo the purse snap and remove the locking discs. From the right side, insert the prongs of one half through the slits in one piece of lining, attaching one piece of acetate on the wrong side *(diag 5)*.

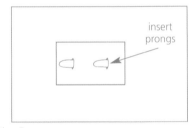

insert prongs

Diag 5

Re-position one locking disc over the prongs. Fold the prongs outwards to secure *(diag 6)*.

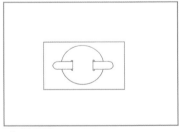

Diag 6

Repeat for the remaining piece of lining.

3. Constructing the lining

With right sides together and matching raw edges, place the lining pieces together.

Pin and stitch along the sides and base, leaving an 8cm (3 ⅛") opening along the base *(diag 7)*. Press the seams open.

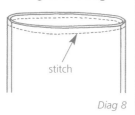

Diag 7

4. Attaching the lining to the bag

Matching upper raw edges and side seams, place the lining over the bag. Pin and stitch along the upper edge *(diag 8)*.

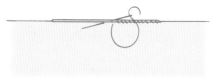

Diag 8

Turn the lining to the right side through the opening in the base. Hand stitch the opening closed *(diag 9)*.

Diag 9

Position the lining inside the bag and gently press the upper edge, avoiding the beads.

5. Finishing

Make the beaded fringe and handle following the instructions on pages 96 - 97.

KEEPSAKE

For color photos and full details see pages 100 - 105

CUTTING OUT

Where pattern pieces are not provided, cut the pieces according to the following measurements.

Garter: cut one, 14cm x 105cm wide (5 ½" x 41 ¼")

Horseshoe: cut one, 14cm x 105cm wide (5 ½" x 41 ¼")

Bag cord: cut two on the bias, each 45cm x 4cm wide (17 ¾" x 1 ½")

Bag base: cut three circles, each 12cm diameter (4 ¾")

CUTTING LAYOUT

Silk dupioni

1. Garter
2. Horseshoe
3. Bag
4. Bag base and lining
5. Bag petal fronts
6. Bag cord

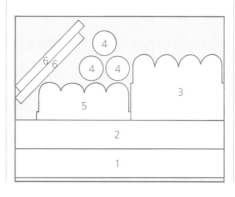

CONSTRUCTION

All seam allowances are 1cm (⅜") unless otherwise specified. The shaded areas on the following diagrams indicate the right side of the fabric.

GARTER

1. Forming the garter

With right sides together, fold the silk dupioni in half along the length. Beginning and ending 5cm (2") from the ends, stitch along the long side. Turn the tube to the right side and press so the seam is 2cm (¾") from the upper edge *(diag 1)*.

Diag 1

Press under the seam allowance on the unstitched sections.

With right sides together and matching ends, pin and stitch the two ends together *(diag 2)*.

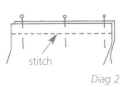

Diag 2

Press the seam allowance open.

2. Forming the casing

Form a casing for the elastic by sewing two seams along the length of the tube, one 7mm (⁵⁄₁₆") from the upper fold and the other 2.5cm (1") from the lower fold *(diag 3)*.

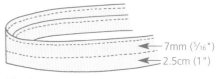

7mm (⁵⁄₁₆")
2.5cm (1")

Diag 3

3. Attaching the beads

On the right side, secure pearl beads along the lower stitchline at 1.5cm (⅝") intervals.

4. Inserting the elastic

Thread the elastic through the casing. Overlap the ends of the elastic by 1cm (⅜").

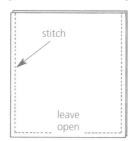

Securely stitch the ends together *(diag 4)*.

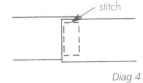

Diag 4

Close the opening with handstitching. Distribute the gathers evenly around the garter.

Work the embroidery following the instructions in the article.

HORSESHOE

1. Preparation

Trace the horseshoe template onto the cardboard or plastic and cut out.

Fold the silk dupioni in half along the length and stitch along the long side. Turn the tube to the right side and press so the seam is 2cm (³⁄₄") from the upper edge *(diag 1)*.

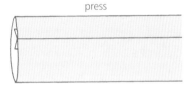

press

Diag 1

Turn in the seam allowances at each end and press. Machine stitch across one end as close as possible to the edge of the folded fabric *(diag 2)*.

stitch

Diag 2

2. Gathering the fabric

Stitch two rows of gathering along the tube, positioning one 7mm (⁵⁄₁₆") from the upper edge and the other 2.5cm (1") from the lower edge *(diag 3)*.

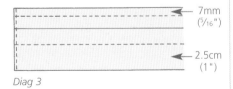

7mm (⁵⁄₁₆")

2.5cm (1")

Diag 3

Feed the fabric onto the horseshoe shape and pull up the gathering threads to fit.

Tie off the gathering and handstitch the open end closed. Distribute the gathers evenly around the horseshoe.

3. Preparing the ribbon

Measure up 25cm (10") from each end of the satin ribbon and mark with pins. Beginning at one pin and working towards the end, attach pearl beads along the ribbon at 8mm (⁵⁄₁₆") intervals. Repeat on the other end.

Fold five loops, each 2.5cm (1") long, at one end of the ribbon, ensuring the pearl beads face outwards. Fan the loops slightly and position them behind one end. Handstitch in place *(diag 4)*.

stitch

Diag 4

Repeat for the remaining end of the ribbon.

Fold the ribbon to find the center. Fold three loops each 2cm (³⁄₄") long. Secure the loops by taking 2 - 3 stitches through them at the base. Thread a diamante flower and then a pearl bead onto the needle. Take the needle back through the diamante flower only and through the ribbon to the other side. Thread a second diamante flower and pearl bead onto the needle. Take the needle back through the diamante and ribbon. End off the thread behind the first diamante flower *(diag 5)*.

Diag 5

Attach pearl beads at 4cm (1 ½") intervals along the ribbon, securing one on each side at exactly the same position. When attaching the third pair of beads from the looped center, take the thread through both sections of the ribbon to join them together *(diag 6)*.

Diag 6

This forms a wrist loop. Work the embroidery following the instructions in the article.

BAG

1. Preparation

After cutting out the pieces, transfer the embroidery design to the petal fronts and work the embroidery.

2. Sewing the side seam

Join the bag into a cylinder using a French seam *(diag 1)*. Press the seam flat.

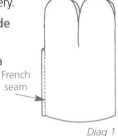

French seam

Diag 1

3. Joining the side to the base

Tack two layers of the base together. These will be treated as one layer from now on. Mark the base into quarters with pins. Begining at the seam, divide the lower edge of the bag into quarters and mark with pins. Stitch two rows of gathering around the lower edge of the bag *(diag 2)*.

gathering

Diag 2

Pull up the gathering until it fits the base. With right sides together, pin the gathered edge to the base, matching quarter marks and distributing the gathers evenly. Stitch *(diag 3)*. Press the seam allowance towards the base.

stitch

Diag 3

On the right side, mark the edge of the base into six equal sections. Sew a large crystal at each mark *(diag 4)*.

crystals

Diag 4

Work a buttonhole at the position indicated on the pattern *(diag 5)*. Work a second buttonhole on the opposite side of the bag.

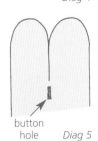

button hole

Diag 5

4. Attaching the base lining

Stay stitch around the base lining along the stitchline. Press the seam allowance to the wrong side, clipping where necessary (diag 6).

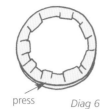

press   Diag 6

Place a 10cm (4") diameter circle of cardboard or plastic onto the base of the bag, tucking it under the pressed seam allowance (diag 7).

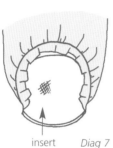

insert   Diag 7

With the right side facing up, place the lining over the cardboard. Pin and handstitch in place.

5. Attaching the petal fronts

Fold up the extending section of each lace motif and pin in place. This prevents them from being caught in the seam.

With right sides together and aligning raw edges, stitch the side seam of the petal section. Press the seam open. With right sides together and aligning raw edges, pin and tack the petal fronts to the petal shapes on the bag. Stitch, using a 3mm (⅛") seam allowance.

Reinforce the sections between the petals (diag 8). Clip into the reinforced corners. Turn to the right side, carefully pushing out the petals. Press along the seam only.

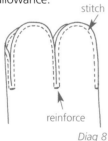

stitch

reinforce

Diag 8

6. Making the casing

Turn under 1cm (⅜") along the straight edge of the petal fronts. Pin and tack the folded edge to the inside of the bag (diag 9). Stitch as close as possible to the folded edge.

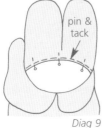

pin & tack

Diag 9

Stitch again 2.5cm (1") above the first stitchline, ensuring the buttonholes are centered between stitchlines.

7. Finishing the petals

Beginning and ending at the base of one petal, topstitch around the petals 6mm (¼") from the edge (diag 10). Unpin the lace motifs.

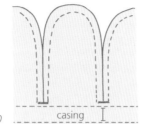

Diag 10   casing

Attach pearl beads to the front and back of the petals along the stitchlines, positioning them 1cm (⅜") apart. Using the photograph as a guide, stitch the pearl beads and crystals to the lower section of each lace motif. Evenly space four crystals along the lower section of the stitchline.

8. Making the cord

With right sides together, fold one bias strip in half along the length. Pin and stitch. Turn through to the right side and press. Repeat for the second strip.

9. Finishing

Thread one length of cord through the casing, beginning and ending through the one opening (diag 11). Beginning and ending at the other opening, repeat for the second length of cord.

Diag 11

On one side, tie the ends of the cord together in a firm knot. Trim any excess length beyond the knot (diag 12). Repeat for the other cord. Attach pearl beads over the knots.

trim   Diag 12

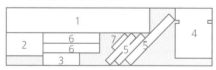

PURPLE PASSION

For color photos and full details see pages 106 - 109

CUTTING OUT

Trace pattern pieces A, B and C onto lightweight interfacing or tracing paper, transferring the pattern markings. Where pattern pieces are not provided, cut the pieces according to the measurements below.

Cut out all pieces following the cutting layouts.

Silk dupioni

Front insert: cut one, 13cm x 65cm wide (5 ⅛" x 25 ⅝")

Front insert backing: cut one, 12cm x 20cm wide (4 ¾" x 8")

Piping: cut two on the bias, 20cm x 4cm wide (8" x 1½") and one 36cm x 4cm wide (14 ⅛" x 1½")

Straps: cut two, 31cm x 5cm wide (12 ¼" x 2")

Button loop: cut one on the bias, 10cm x 2.5cm wide (4" x 1")

CUTTING LAYOUT

Silk dupioni
1. Front insert
2. Front insert backing
3. Upper front band (A)
4. Lower front and back (B)
5. Piping
6. Straps
7. Button loop

Satin lining

8. Lining (C)

Wadding

3. Upper front band (A)

4. Lower front and back (B)

CONSTRUCTION

All seam allowances are 1.5cm (⅝") unless otherwise specified.

1. Blocking and shaping the smocking

Remove the pleating threads except for the upper and lower holding rows. Place the smocked insert face up on the ironing board. Ensuring the iron does not touch the smocking, pin and steam the smocking to fit the width of the insert lining. Leave pinned to the ironing board until dry.

2. Backing the insert

With wrong sides together and aligning raw edges at the sides, place the insert onto the insert backing. Keeping the pleats straight and even, baste through all layers (diag 1).

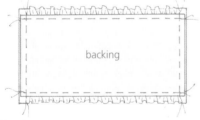

Diag 1

3. Making the piping

Lay the piping cord along one piping strip on the wrong side. Fold the fabric over the cord, matching raw edges. Stitch close to the cord (diag 2). Trim the seam allowance to 1.5cm (⅝"). Repeat for the remaining pieces.

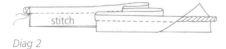

Diag 2

4. Piping the front insert

Pin one short piece of piping to the upper edge of the insert with the corded edge aligned with the top of the beads.

Pin the remaining short length to the lower edge of the insert in the same manner. Tack and stitch both lengths of piping in place along the piping stitchline (diag 3).

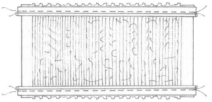

Diag 3

Trim the seam allowances on the upper and lower edges to 1.5cm (⅝").

5. Attaching the wadding

Fuse the wadding to the wrong side of the upper front band and the lower front and back piece.

6. Attaching the front upper band

With right sides together and matching raw edges, pin the band to the upper edge of the insert. Stitch the layers together, stitching between the previous piping stitch line and the corded edge of the piping (diag 4).

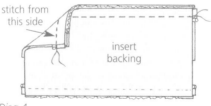

stitch from this side

insert backing

Diag 4

Trim the seam to 8mm (⁵⁄₁₆") and press the band away from the smocked insert.

7. Attaching the lower front and back

With right sides together and matching raw edges, pin the lower front to the lower edge of the insert. Stitch in the same manner as the upper band.

Trim the seam to 8mm (⁵⁄₁₆") and press the lower front away from the smocked insert (diag 5).

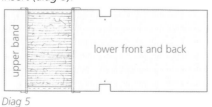

upper band

lower front and back

Diag 5

8. Side seams

With right sides together and matching top and side edges, fold the bag in half. Pin the front to the back at the sides. Stitch the side seams, ensuring the beads are not caught in the stitching (diag 6).

stitch

Diag 6

Trim the seams to 8mm (⁵⁄₁₆") and press towards the back.

9. Shaping the base

With right sides together and matching raw edges, fold the cut-out section at the base of the bag so that the seam is aligned with the mark on the opposite edge of the base. Pin and stitch across the end on the marked stitchlines (diag 7).

stitch

side seam

Diag 7

Trim the seam to 8mm (⁵⁄₁₆"). Form the opposite corner in the same manner.

Turn the bag to the right side.

10. Piping the upper edge

Beginning at the center back with a 1cm (⅜") tail extending, pin the remaining length of piping around the upper edge. At the center back, overlap the ends and curve them into the seam allowance. Trim any excess length of piping. Stitch along the piping stitchline (diag 8).

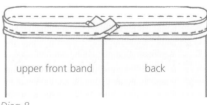

upper front band

back

Diag 8

11. Button loop

Fold the rectangle for the loop in half down the length. Beginning with a funnel shape and tapering towards the foldline, stitch 6mm (¼") from the fold. Restitch the seam to reinforce *(diag 9)*.

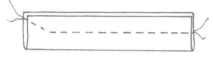

Diag 9

Turn the loop through with a loop turner and press. Cut the loop to measure 7.5cm (3"), trimming the wider end off. Fold the loop in half and pin in place at the center of the upper front band *(diag 10)*.

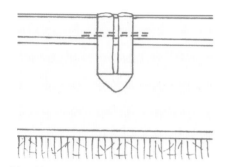

Diag 10

12. Straps

Placing the stitching 1cm (⅜") from the fold, make the straps in the same manner as the button loop. Cut each strap to measure 30cm (11 ¾") long.

Pin the ends of each strap at the marked positions on the upper edge of the bag. Stitch firmly in place *(diag 11)*.

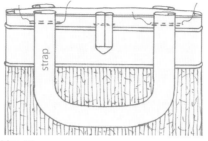

Diag 11

Turn the bag inside out.

13. Lining

With right sides together and matching raw edges, pin the front to the back at the sides. Stitch, leaving an 8cm (3 ⅛") opening in one side seam. Trim the seams to 8mm (⁵⁄₁₆") and press towards the back. Fold and stitch the base shaping in the same manner as the bag. Turn the lining to the right side.

Place the lining inside the bag. With right sides together, pin the lining to the upper edge of the bag. Stitch the layers together, stitching between the previous piping stitch line and the corded edge of the piping *(diag 12)*.

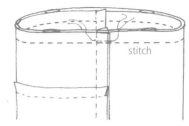

Diag 12

Trim the seam to 8mm (⁵⁄₁₆").

Turn the bag and lining to the right side through the opening in the lining. Fold in the seam allowances on the opening and topstitch the edges together close to the fold *(diag 13)*.

Diag 13

Place the lining inside the bag. Carefully press the lining around the upper edge.

14. Finishing

Cover the button following the manu-facturers instructions. Attach it to the upper edge of the back to correspond with the button loop *(diag 14)*.

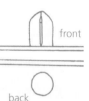

CONTRIBUTORS

Many thanks to all the contributors to this beautiful book

ANNA SCOTT ~ *Beaded Flower*

DANA COX ~ *Pearls of Wisdom*

JULIE GRAUE ~ *Dare to Dream*

DEBORAH WEST BANGS ~ *Nostalgia*

ANNIE HUMPHRIS ~ *Silken Touch*

CAROLYN PEARCE ~ *Glad Tidings* AND *Rejoice*

LIZ VICKERY ~ *Antique Gold* AND *Rare Vintage*

JAN KERTON ~ *Berry Delight*

CHRISTINE BISHOP ~ *Veil of Gold*

LESLEY TURPIN-DELPORT ~ *Winter Love*

KAREN TORRISI ~ *Glittering Dreams*

SUSAN O'CONNOR ~ *Caprice*

HELAN PEARCE ~ *Taking Tea*

HELEN ERIKSSON ~ *Keepsake*

CORAL MOSS ~ *Purple Passion*

THE BEADED FLOWER
Attaching beads
Individually sewn bead 8
Attaching with a second bead 8
Lazy squaw stitch 8
Couched beads 9
Couched beads over a cord 9
Overlapping sequins 9

PEARLS OF WISDOM
Attaching beads 13

DARE TO DREAM
Beaded button 17

NOSTALGIA
Mitered ribbon leaf 22
Wild rose 23
Cabochon rose 24
Continuous petal fower 25

SILKEN TOUCH
Making a twisted cord 29

ANTIQUE GOLD
Beading 38
Working with lengths of beads 38
Beading a leaf 39

BERRY DELIGHT
Making a strawberry 45
Making a large blackberry 46
Making a blueberry 46
Making a small blackberry 47
Making a mulberry 47
Making a red currant 47

VEIL OF GOLD
Dressing a slate frame 51

WINTER LOVE
Needlewoven bar 57
Spent flower 58

GLITTERING DREAMS
Pink flower 63
Apricot flower 63

CAPRICE
Yellow berries 70
Small blue flower spray 70
Large pink flower 71
Attaching the frame to the bag 72

REJOICE
Armenian edging stitch 79
Basque stitch 79
Breton stitch 80
Cross stitch flower 81
Knotted cable chain 82
Raised cross stitch flower 82
Whipped reverse chain stitch 83

TAKING TEA
Palestrina stitch 90
Detached petal 91

RARE VINTAGE
Cluster 98
Handle 99

KEEPSAKE
Gathered ribbon rose 105

PURPLE PASSION
Beaded alternating cable 109